Best Practices of Online Education

A Guide for Christian Higher Education

Best Practices of Online Education

A Guide for Christian Higher Education

edited by

Mark A. Maddix
Northwest Nazarene University

James R. Estep
Lincoln Christian University

Mary E. Lowe
Erskine Theological Seminary

INFORMATION AGE PUBLISHING, INC.
Charlotte, NC • www.infoagepub.com

Library of Congress Cataloging-in-Publication Data

Best practices of online education : a guide for Christian higher education
/ edited by Mark A. Maddix, Northwest Nazarene University, James R. Estep,
Lincoln Christian University, Mary E. Lowe, Erskine Theological Seminary.
    pages cm
 Includes bibliographical references.
 ISBN 978-1-61735-768-8 (pbk.) – ISBN 978-1-61735-769-5 (hardcover) –
ISBN 978-1-61735-770-1 (ebook)
1. Christian universities and colleges–United States–Data processing. 2.
Computer-assisted instruction–United States. I. Maddix, Mark A., 1965- II.
Estep, James Riley, 1963- III. Lowe, Mary Ella.
 LB2395.7.B47 2012
 371.33'40973–dc23

                                                          2012000584

Dedicated to Dr. Ted Ward, educator, innovator, and colleague in Christian education.

CONTENTS

Preface ix

SECTION I

THEORETICAL AND THEOLOGICAL FOUNDATIONS
OF ONLINE EDUCATION

1 Educational Theory and Online Education 3
   Mark H. Heinemann and James Riley Estep Jr.

2 Adult Learning Theory and Online Learning 17
   Stephen D. Lowe

3 Developing Online Learning Communities 31
   Mark A. Maddix

4 Social Presence in Online Learning 41
   Stephen Kemp

5 Spiritual Formation as Whole-Person Development in Online
   Education 55
   Mary E. Lowe

6 Challenges and Opportunities for Online Theological
   Education 65
   James Riley Estep Jr. and Steven Yates

SECTION II

GENERATING AND FACILITATING EFFECTIVE LEARNING IN ONLINE EDUCATION

7 Best Practices in Online Teaching 81
C. Damon Osborne

8 Visualize More: Effective Online Teaching Methods 91
Jay Richard Akkerman

9 Characteristics of Successful Online Students 101
Jason D. Baker

10 Generating and Facilitating Effective Online Discussion 107
Mark A. Maddix

11 Online Faculty Development 121
Dale Hale

SECTION III

DEVELOPING AND ASSESSING ONLINE COURSES AND PROGRAMS

12 Evaluating Course Management Systems 131
Eric Kellerer

13 Developing Effective Infrastructures for Online Programs 139
Gregory W. Bourgond

14 Developing Online Programs 147
David M. Phillips

15 Online Program and Curriculum Mapping 155
Christine Bauer and Mary Jones

16 Online Course Design Considerations 163
Christine Bauer and Mary Jones

17 Assessing Online Learning 173
Meri MacLeod

About the Editors 183

About the Contributors 187

PREFACE

SURFING

This summer, my wife and I (Mark Maddix) traveled to southern California to visit our son for a few days. During our visit, my son decided to teach me the fine art of surfing. As a veteran explorer of the ocean, I thought my previous experience would be sufficient for learning to navigate the complexities of surfing. My son, an experienced surfer, guided me through the steps and processes. We began the day by gathering our equipment, which included a wet suit and a long surf board. Once our equipment was in place, he taught me how to position my feet on the board and how to lie down and paddle in anticipation of the waves. He illustrated how to get up on the board, something that is harder than I anticipated.

With the instructions in place, I attempted the fine art of surfing. After several attempts, I realized that what I once knew about the ocean was insufficient for mastering the art of surfing. I had to rethink how to approach the waves and how to balance myself on a very quick surfboard. My son continued to encourage and guide me through the process. After a long day of "surfing," if you call partial standing on a board surfing, I was tired and frustrated. I realized surfing required skill and practice to be fun. It took several days of surfing to become comfortable on my board, but eventually I began to enjoy the excitement that comes from gliding through the ocean.

In many ways, surfing is a good metaphor for navigating the turbulent waters of online education. Online education requires having the right equipment, knowing the right processes and procedures, and developing the right skills through continual practice. Some teachers and administrators develop online courses and programs without developing the appro-

Best Practices of Online Education, pages ix–xiii
Copyright © 2012 by Information Age Publishing

priate infrastructures to support online education. The result is frustrated students and teachers. Effective online teaching and learning requires educational theories and practices. Online education requires proper training and development of teachers in how to develop online courses and how to understand the online student. Even the most experienced teacher can become frustrated without the proper training in these new waters. Both for the novice and the expert, guidelines are necessary.

CHRISTIAN HIGHER EDUCATION

The landscape of Christian higher education is changing. Students once spent most of their time in a traditional classroom with a professor, but now they take online and hybrid courses (face to face and online). Some students complete their entire degree in a fully online program.

As the demand for online courses and programs increase, teachers and administrators in Christian universities and seminaries face new challenges. Many teachers and administrators feel the pressure to launch online courses and programs without adequate training and resources. They lack the expertise in online course development, understanding of online students, and knowledge of how to generate and facilitate effective online learning. They struggle with knowing how to provide appropriate infrastructures, such as choosing the right Course Management Systems (CMS) and emerging technologies. Some teachers and administrators still believe online education is inferior to traditional face-to-face learning. Others question the whole online enterprise.

This book addresses the challenges teachers and administrators face in offering online courses and programs in Christian higher education. The book is designed to assist Christian teachers and administrators to understand how to generate and facilitate effective learning in online education. We have titled this book *Best Practices of Online Education: A Guide for Christian Higher Education* because it combines the best research and practices in the field of online education with a theological framework for understanding online learning. Experts and practitioners who have developed online programs and taught online courses for many years wrote this book.

The book is unique because it approaches online education from a Christian perspective. This means the book is designed to facilitate discussion and dialogue among Christian educators about the challenges and opportunities of offering online classes and programs in a Christian context. The book also addresses the opportunities that Christian universities and seminaries have in offering online courses and programs. For example, some Christian educators still contend that Christian education cannot take place online because persons can only be formed and shaped through traditional face-to-face courses and programs. However, we give evidence of how students' faith can be formed and shaped through intentional online learning communities.

We divide the book into three sections. The first provides theoretical and theological foundations of online education. Section II focuses on exploring and generating effective learning in online education. Section III gives guidance in developing and assessing online courses and programs.

In Chapter 1, James Estep and Mark Heinemann argue that a constructivist educational approach is needed for effective online teaching and learning. They give practical essentials of educational theory and processes that focus on the aim, content, teacher, learner, environment, evaluation, methods, and Triune God. In Chapter 2, Stephen Lowe provides both a theological and educational framework for understanding adult learners. He includes characteristics of adult learners based on Malcolm Knowles' theory of andragogy and current research in contextualized and situated models of adult learning. In Chapter 3, Mark Maddix expresses the importance of developing community in online courses. Maddix indicates that effective online learning takes place in supportive learning communities, which is especially important in fostering personal and spiritual formation. He concludes the chapter with a list of best practices in online learning communities. In Chapter 4, Stephen Kemp focuses on the research and practice of how transactional distance can be broken in online courses and how social presence can be optimized in online and real life social contexts. He includes a list of best practices for developing social presence in online courses. In Chapter 5, Mary Lowe addresses the question of whether persons can be spiritually formed in online courses. Based on developmental psychology, she develops an ecosystem of spiritual formation that includes the whole person. Human ecology theories tell us that whole person development (intellectual, social, moral, emotional, psychological, and spiritual) is instigated through social interactions through the continuum of our ecosystems. In Chapter 6, James Estep and Steven Yates explore the challenges and opportunities of online education in Christian universities and seminaries. They discuss such issues as financial considerations and online infrastructures. They also discuss the challenges of training faculty who are technologically challenged. They explore concerns expressed by alumni and collegial perceptions.

The second section of the book focuses on exploring and generating effective learning in online education. In Chapter 7, Damon Osborne provides a list of best practices in online teaching. These practices include preparing the course prior to teaching the course, establishing social presence in the online course, facilitating effectively, maintaining boundaries between online work and life, and bringing closure to an online course. These practices provide the online teacher with techniques for effective online teaching. In Chapter 8, Jay Akkerman encourages online educators to develop online courses that appeal to the students' visual capacities. He gives a historical and theological basis for how the Church used visual art and icons to communicate Christian ideas before printing was the norm. Effective online courses use a variety of visual components. In Chapter 9, Jason Baker addresses the theological foundations of students as image bearers of God. He provides practical advice for how students can succeed in online courses. This includes technological literacy, strong reading skills, the ability to communicate effectively in writing, good time management, and being an independent and autonomous learner. In Chapter 10, Mark Maddix discusses how to generate and facilitate effective online discussion. He uses the Community of Inquiry Model (CIM) to evaluate student learning in online discussion. He provides best practices for online discussion, such as developing clear guidelines and expectations for discussion, developing a discussion board rubric, facilitating discussion on a regular basis, developing assignments that encourage active learning, and generating good questions for discussion. In Chapter 11, Dale Hale focuses on the importance of providing continual training for online teachers. He argues that institutions need to have a training and development plan for online teachers.

The third section of the book gives guidance in developing and assessing online courses and programs. In Chapter 12, Eric Kellerer gives an overview of the process of selecting a Course Management System (CMS) based on the institution's context and program needs. He provides a list of preliminary questions to ask when institutions are considering purchasing a CMS. In Chapter 13, Gregory Bourgond explores the importance of developing consistent standards, protocols, organization, and planning for online programs. These online program infrastructure considerations ensure the consistency and coherence of online course and program offerings. In Chapter 14, David Phillips gives practical advice for developing online programs. He argues that the mission of offering online programs is to be consistent with the mission of the Christian university and seminary. He also illustrates the importance for institutions to consider the investment in developing online programs by understanding learning theory, online technology, adult learners, and curricular design. He concludes by focusing on the importance of developing supportive structures such as student services, financial aid, registration, and academic support for online students. In Chapters 15 and 16, Christine Bauer and Mary Jones focus on curriculum mapping and course design. They argue that once an institution decides to launch an online program, it is important to develop a curriculum map to ensure effective learning. Program development includes the establishment of program learning outcomes based on institutional and national standards. They recommend a Course Development Team (CDT) consisting of experts in instructional design and content to develop the online course. In Chapter 17, Meri MacLeod focuses on developing learning assessments for online courses. She shows how new interactive media can enhance student learning and expand the types of assessment available for the teacher. She provides such assessment strategies as developing rubrics, collaborative assessments, peer review, and self-reflection.

We hope this book provides teachers and administrators with a practical guide for developing effective online courses and programs. We believe this book provides both a theoretical and practical framework for generating and facilitating online education. As you read this book, it is our prayer that you will be inspired to embrace the excitement of engaging in online education.

Mark A. Maddix
James R. Estep
Mary E. Lowe
Editors

SECTION I

THEORETICAL AND THEOLOGICAL FOUNDATIONS
OF ONLINE EDUCATION

CHAPTER 1

EDUCATIONAL THEORY AND ONLINE EDUCATION

Mark H. Heinemann
Dallas Theological Seminary

James Riley Estep Jr.
Lincoln Christian University

Have you ever been a foreigner? Inexperienced visitors to other countries may find some things to be vaguely familiar but find others to be strange. In every arena of life—language, social customs, cuisine, transportation— even experienced travelers know they are not at home. In a similar way, first-time teachers in an online learning environment may feel disoriented. They are still teachers engaged in the task of educating students, but they are also "strangers in a strange land." Online education challenges widely-held educational assumptions and casts the traditional skills associated with teaching in a different light.

This chapter intends to help those considering or beginning teaching online by briefly introducing the theory and practice of this strange new mode of education. To do this, we will take off from the technological revolution and ascend over certain presuppositions and selected learning theories as they relate to online instruction. From there we will point to certain ele-

Best Practices of Online Education, pages 3–16

ments and processes at work in effective online instruction, hopefully landing at an initial overview of the terrain, with our guidebook firmly in hand.

THE REVOLUTIONARY MESSAGE
OF TECHNOLOGICAL MEDIA

Marshall McLuhan is famous for coining the phrase "the medium is the message." This often-misunderstood statement means that each medium or technology, regardless of the content it mediates, has its own intrinsic effects that are its unique message.

> The "message" of any medium or technology is the change of scale or pace or pattern that it introduces into human affairs. The railway did not introduce movement or transportation or wheel or road into human society, but it accelerated and enlarged the scale of previous human functions, creating totally new kinds of cities and new kinds of work and leisure. This happened whether the railway functioned in a tropical or northern environment, and is quite independent of the freight or content of the railway medium. (McLuhan, 1964, p. 8)

What McLuhan writes about the railroad applies with equal validity to the media of print, television, computers, and now the Internet. The medium is the message "because it is the medium that shapes and controls the scale and form of human association and action" (McLuhan, 1964, p. 9).

The way that the online learning environment shapes the method and message of the teacher is an excellent example of this phenomenon. New online instructors must realize that they are not just embarking upon a new way of doing old things. Rather, they are venturing down a revolutionary path in which new media have so shaped and shifted the "scale and form of human association and action" that teaching and learning are, at times, almost unrecognizable. Just as moving in the past few decades from chalkboards to whiteboards to overheads to computer presentations and to smart boards has changed both how and what we teach, so the advent of the Internet is changing the shape of education.

PRESUPPOSITIONS ABOUT ONLINE EDUCATION

In order to accomplish our task in this brief scope, we come with some important presuppositions. First, it is assumed that we approach this subject from a Christian point of view. This can sound trite until we observe certain important consequences of this approach, noted below. For now let us say that our faith perspective should profoundly impact what, how, and why we do *any form* of teaching and learning. Christian education remains Christian by its theological orientation and assumptions, not by the methods of delivery.

Second, it is assumed that the distance in distance education does *not* fundamentally change the *nature* of the teaching/learning process, in all of its variety, complexity, and mystery. Of course, the options for the *application* of our theories of education *will be* changed by the separation of teacher and learner in time and space. Still, though online education may reflect some of the consequences foreseen by McLuhan, we believe the digital classroom can be a place of significant learning. After approvingly citing Richard Clark's strong warnings against becoming "enamored with the toys of technology," Bernard, et al. go on to assert: "Instead, it is the characteristics of instructional design, such as the instructional strategies used, the feedback provided, and the degree of learner engagement, that create the conditions within which purposive learning will occur" (2004, p. 411).

Third, it is assumed that the primary value of distance education is not as a replacement for local, face-to-face teaching and learning. Rather, it is a set of possible strategies, which can be used by an educational institution to overcome a temporary or long-term separation between the teacher and prospective students. At its core, the goal of distance education is to increase access, not to compete with the traditional mode. Though much research over the last 25 years has attempted to compare the two with regard to outcomes, satisfaction, and the like, the results have varied widely and remain inconclusive. Bernard et al.'s (2004) careful meta-analysis of research from 1985 through 2002 is just one of many studies to have reached this same basic conclusion.

Fourth, it is assumed that most schools cannot afford to lag behind in offering quality online education as an option for promising students unable, for one reason or another, to participate in traditional programs. As the online option grows in convenience and perceived value, only the most elite institutions will be able to ignore it—for a while. It is unfortunate, but it is likely that institutions that do not engage in online education will eventually be viewed as antiquated, like a scroll in a library full of books. Maintaining *status quo* is no longer the *status quo*. The fact is that the online education revolution is not coming . . . it is already here. We believe our attitude should be a healthy opportunism like that of de Tocqueville as he observed the "social revolution" of democracy in America:

> I have not even affected to discuss whether the social revolution, which I believe to be irresistible, is advantageous or prejudicial to mankind; I have acknowledged this revolution as a fact already accomplished or on the eve of its accomplishment; and I have selected the nation, from amongst those which have undergone it, in which its development has been the most peaceful and the most complete, in order to discern its natural consequences, and, if it be possible, to distinguish the means by which it may be rendered profitable. (de Tocqueville, 1835/1966, p. xlvii)

Fifth, it is assumed that our current students are not the same as those of yesterday. Already a decade ago, educational futurist Marc Prensky (2001) famously described today's students as Digital Natives and today's teachers as Digital Immigrants "... who speak an outdated language (that of the pre-digital age), [and] are struggling to teach a population that speaks an entirely new language" (2001, n.p.). Innovations have always had natives (the early adopters) and immigrants (the later adopters), but the growing generation gap produced by the constant and ever more rapid change, particularly in electronic technologies, surpasses in scale and pace anything that has gone before.

LEARNING THEORIES AND ONLINE EDUCATION

This chapter is not the place to craft a theoretical basis for the online mode of education. We can, however look at aspects of some general educational theories as they relate to online education. Added to this, we can also delve briefly into some of the theorizing that has been taking place among distance learning experts.

Salient Aspects of Existing Educational Theories—Two Examples

It is important at this point to recognize that most educational theories are adaptable to the online environment. This goes back to our presupposition above that the nature of teaching and learning remains the same regardless of time and place. The two examples below have been chosen because of their current influence on distance education.

Constructivism. Liu and Matthews (2005) write that since the 1970s, "constructivism"—basically a theory of learning traceable at least as far back as Piaget—"has been the buzzword in school education and teacher training in the western part of the world" (p. 386). This broad spectrum of theory/paradigm/philosophy/teaching method has also been enthusiastically embraced as the dominant approach to understanding learning in online education.

Noting the fragmentation and confusion among its advocates, Baviskar, Hartle, and Whitney (2009) offer four criteria gleaned from the literature that characterize the constructivist teaching-learning process, as follows. First, new knowledge is constructed as it relates to the prior knowledge of the learner. Second, cognitive dissonance between prior knowledge and new knowledge stimulates learning. Third, application of new knowledge, accompanied by feedback, enables the learner to check its validity and to build connections with an ever-increasing variety of contexts. Finally, for maximum impact a learner should be enabled to reflect upon and express what he or she has learned (Baviskar, Hartle, & Whitney, 2009).

From the point of view of many online educators, there is nothing new here. Certainly there can be agreement with Phillips (1995) on the positive contributions of this approach, namely an emphasis on the necessity for active participation by the learner, together with the recognition of the social nature of learning. Added to a list of positive aspects of constructivism could be the emphasis on a learner-centered rather than a teacher-centered approach. On the negative side, radical constructivists tend toward philosophical and methodological positions that are unacceptable to the biblical faith, for example, epistemological relativism, the rejection of divine revelation, and so on.

Bloom's Taxonomy of Educational Objectives. Benjamin J. Bloom and his colleagues (1956) developed what has been the standard taxonomy of the cognitive domain of learning for over fifty years. Bloom's model postulates six levels of cognitive processing, each with descriptors that help identify the extent of a learner's engagement with and progress in learning a subject. The age of this tool testifies to its usefulness, but the descriptors reflect a traditional classroom environment.

Additional new tangible markers are being developed, reflecting the use of computer and Internet technologies. Andrew Churches' (2008) work on "digital verbs" is one example of this. These updated verbs are not replacements for Bloom's original descriptors, but are meant to be additions that reflect the digital culture that has risen over the past 30 years (see Figure 1.1).

Cognitive Domain		"Digital Verbs" describing the level of attainment
6	Evaluation	Programming, filming, blog/vlog designing, publishing, v-casting, producing/directing, wiki-ing, animating, mix/re-mixing
5	Synthesis	Blog/vlog, commenting, reviewing, posting, collaborating, moderating, networking, refactoring, α/β testing
4	Analysis	Mashing, linking, tagging, validating, reverse-engineering, cracking
3	Application	Running, loading, playing, operating, hacking, uploading, sharing, editing
2	Comprehension	Advanced searches, blog-journaling, twittering, categorizing, subscribing, annotating
1	Knowledge	Bullet pointing, highlighting, bookmarking, social networking, searching/googling

Figure 1.1 Digital Bloom Taxonomy.

Distance Education Theories—Two Examples

Distance Education experts have put forth theories attempting to explain the mysteries of their mode of teaching and learning. Once again, two examples will be presented, chosen according to their current influence in the field.

Transactional Distance Theory. Michael G. Moore's theory of "transactional distance" intends to provide a broad theoretical framework for the pedagogy of distance education and has established itself as one of the most discussed theories of the field. Research results have been, however, inconclusive (Giossos, Koutsouba, Lionarakis, & Skavantzos, 2009). To summarize, Moore asserts that transactional distance (the psychological and communication gap between instructor and student) is reduced by dialogue (two-way communication between instructor and student), and increased by too little or too much structure (the extent to which the teacher controls the process). Also, student autonomy (the extent to which the student controls the teaching-learning process) increases or decreases in synch with transactional distance (Moore & Kearsley, 2011).

Setting aside for a moment the empirical support for or against the theory, there are certain helpful insights that can be gleaned from it. For example: (a) the importance of facilitating two-way communication to maximize instructor-student understanding; (b) the need for structure, but not rigidity; and (c) the need for student autonomy, but only as long as it serves student learning, and never without ongoing supervision.

Connectivism. Downes and Siemens started a vigorous conversation in 2005 with their ideas on what has come to be called connectivism (Bell, 2011). Reminiscent of certain aspects of Illich's (1970) "deschooling" ideas from a previous era, connectivism sees learning as a matter of life-long cycling through one's personal network of learning communities, both as a provider and receptor of knowledge (Kop & Hill, 2008). Today's technology-based capacity to find, know, share, diversify, compare, correct, and store knowledge is now beyond anything the "deschoolers" could have imagined, and is thus that much more compelling as a framework for life-long learning.

As we have seen with the other examples of theorizing above, there is nothing really new in connectivism except the media-induced McLuhan-type message of shifts of "scale and form of human association and action" that have been making their way across the globe for the past few decades. Perhaps in time, the practice of online education may lead to some radically new theorizing. But for now, the real action centers on the application and adaptation of existing educational wisdom to this new environment.

ESSENTIALS OF EFFECTIVE ONLINE LEARNING

What elements must a teacher attempt to coordinate in order to maximize learning? Burgess (1996) suggests six categories to consider: aim, content, teacher, learner, environment, and evaluation. We will add "methods" and "Triune God" to the list used in the discussion of Christian online learning that follows.

Triune God. For the Christian educator, God radically changes the teaching-learning process. A helpful exercise would be to go through each of the categories in this list and ask: How does the working of Triune God affect this part of the teaching-learning process? Downs (1994) helps us get started by suggesting a handful of the major consequences of God's presence in any education calling itself Christian, including online:

> First, we must understand that *unredeemed people cannot understand spiritual truth*... [which] is understood by means of the Holy Spirit.... Second, *there must be supernatural intervention in our ministry for lives to be touched....* When we recognize that unless God is at work our effort is in vain, then we grasp the essential place of prayer.... Third, *Christian education is a partnership between God and the educator*... Christian educators are responsible to teach well and to pray well. (pp. 54–55, emphasis in original)

Aims. As with any course, online instructors must identify the desired learning objectives. For an online course, two additional factors may have to be addressed. First, some form of technology-based objective may need to be established, for example developing a new skill in an area of technology. Second, for the typical online student, often older and in a career, objectives must move beyond content mastery toward the application of content for the life and work of the student.

Content. One common criticism of online education is that content is devalued. This is simply not the case. Students must master the content in order to move beyond it. In addition to the subject-matter content, students must develop increasing information literacy, that is, the ability to do the knowledge networking advocated by the connectivists. Faculty must acknowledge that though they make unique contributions here and there, *most* of what is presented in the classroom is readily accessible elsewhere. For example, teaching a class on Piaget is not the same as writing an article with a unique perspective on his theories—therein lies the instructor's contribution to the content.

Content in online education has two basic dimensions. First, it is communal. It is not contained in the instructor's notebook, with only secondary access provided to students. Rather, the instructor and all the students have access to a common required set of core materials, not to mention access to any other library or Internet resource they may choose to consult. Second, it is personal. Students are encouraged to process the materials for themselves, under the guidance and encouragement of the instructor and within a context faithful to our Christian heritage and convictions.

Learner. Learners who select the option of online education are typically already engaged in life as an adult, for example, having ties to their geographical area, having careers well underway, having families of their own and so on. Such students are likely to try and fit the work for an online course into late evenings, early mornings, coffee breaks—not the ideal times and places. Not surprisingly, studies show that the full lives drawing potential students to the convenience of online learning are often too full to allow a student to finish a course or program of study.

Online learning is not for everyone, but Palloff and Pratt (2003) suggest several things that can be done to help "virtual students" be successful, which we adapt here:

- The virtual student needs to have access to a computer and high-speed connection.
- An online student needs to feel safe in the sense that he or she can be honest about questions, difficulties, and so on.
- Students need to participate with integrity and courtesy in the online environment, in which visual cues are absent.
- Virtual students must be able to manage their lives such that they are able to devote significant, regular time to the course.
- Students need to be or be open to becoming reflective, critical thinkers.

Teacher. As the saying goes in online education circles, a new instructor moves from being "the sage on the stage to a guide on the side." In fact, in high quality distance education programs, the traditional work of the classroom teacher is often divided into four areas: content, instructional design, technology, and instruction. Typically, experts in the various areas build a given course as a team. The best instructors are skilled at fostering student-student and student-instructor interaction. They teach courses already constructed by experts and thus have more time to communicate, encourage, give feedback, build a learning community (see below), and so on.

Moore and Kearsley (2011) suggest that there are four major types of instructor activity, and the first is content management (elaborating course content, supervising and moderating discussions, and supervising projects). Beyond this are activities pertaining to student progress (grading assignments, giving feedback, and keeping records), learner support (helping students manage their study, motivating, answering or referring administrative, technical, and counseling questions, and representing the students with the administration), and finally, evaluating course effectiveness (Moore and Kearsley, 2011). Space does not allow its reproduction here, but the reader is directed to Palloff and Pratt's (2003) excellent chart, "Learner-focused instructional techniques to support online learners" (pp. 13–14).

Environment. A basic distinction to make with online courses is whether the engagement is synchronous or asynchronous. *Synchronous* means that all the students are online at the same time, much like students attending a residential classroom (Figure 1.2). Some online education products allow an instructor to actually see the whole class at once, while the class can see one another and the instructor as well. *Asynchronous* means that students are not simultaneously online with one another. Deadlines and schedules maintain order in the online classroom, but students have the flexibility to post, reply, respond, and do other course requirements by a predetermined time. Most online education courses are taught asynchronously since this format provides the greatest flexibility for the student and instructor.

The idea of a "learning community" has been around for some time, but recently has received more emphasis (Bain, 2004, p. 176). It is simply a fact that we learn more in community than we do in isolation. One of the most effective ways of promoting online community is to build into the beginning of the course a brief time of face-to-face interaction in the form of a block, course, a retreat, or so on (Haythornthwaite, Kazmer, Robins & Shoemaker, 2000).

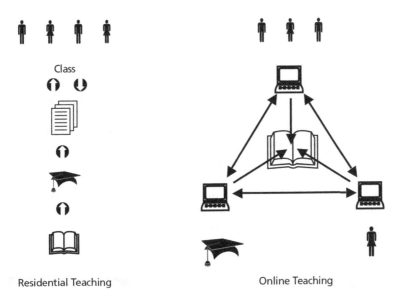

Residential Teaching   Online Teaching

Figure 1.2 Residential versus online learning environments.

A community environment is very desirable in an online course, but can be a challenge to achieve. Brown (2001) reports her own research findings and those of others in this connection (adapted below):

- Modeling, encouragement, and participation by the instructor helped community form more readily in on-line classes.
- Community did not happen unless the participants wanted it to happen.
- Online community was present for some participants and not for others.
- Participants had to get used to the technology, level of content, collaborative interaction, and faceless environment before they could become members of the community.
- Veteran students could help or hinder the formation of community.
- Community could be experienced at different levels.
- Others conferred membership in the on-line community through the acceptance that occurred following participation in a long threaded discussion.
- Voluntary interaction beyond class requirements promoted community.
- Levels of community experienced were closely linked to levels of engagement in the class and dialogue.
- Long-term associations (e.g., through several classes) helped promote community.
- Acceptance and worthiness in the eyes of the on-line community were based more on the quality of a participant's input than on his or her virtual personality.

Instructors are charged with creating a learning environment that creates intellectual excitement combined with clarity and a positive emotional impact flowing from interpersonal rapport with students (Lowman, 1985). Likewise, the best instructors help their students learn in ways that make a sustained, substantial, and positive influence on how those students think, act, and feel (Bain, 2004).

Methods. Online teaching methods usually are not designed for content delivery, but rather to facilitate analysis, synthesis, and evaluation. For example, favored methods might include requiring students to form and defend opinions, to debate options in simulated leadership situations, to respond to case studies and so on. Answering open-ended questions that require students to integrate their insights into a concise response, coupled with faculty and peer interaction, adds breadth and depth to the learning process. Online education also affords a greater opportunity for cross-cultural interaction and collaboration without removing students from their culture or place of service.

Wolcott (1995) suggests the following questions as a guide to choosing methods:

- Am I considering methods because they are familiar and comfortable?
- Are the methods under consideration those that utilize the medium to its best advantage, or are they attempts to reproduce face-to-face instruction?
- What strategies would optimally achieve expectations in light of the variables of students, content, and context?
- What adjustments are required to accommodate instructional activities and visuals to distance delivery?
- Are the methods and techniques likely to encourage participation and interaction?

Citing a number of supporting studies, Heinemann (2007) notes that while many authorities stress the importance of the teacher-student interaction in distance education, "researchers present learner-learner interaction as a very significant factor affecting online learning outcomes, perhaps even the most significant factor" (p. 197). This is a strong reason to facilitate interaction between learners.

As depicted in Figure 1.3, online interaction in a Christian context has additional aspects that are not in the research literature, but are even more

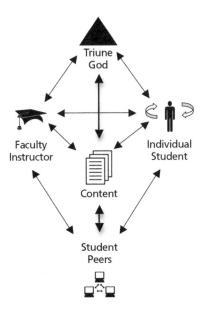

Figure 1.3 Seven-fold interaction.

important. In this case, interaction can be described as seven-fold: (a) God–Instructor, in which the Lord helps the teacher be an example of one taking a godly approach to the subject matter; (b) God–Student, wherein the Lord helps the student learn the content as it relates to His revelation; (c) God–Content, in that "all truth is God's truth" so that He is vitally interested in helping us learn it; (d) Instructor–Student, wherein the instructor leads students by the power of the Spirit toward the predetermined learning objectives; (e) Student–Student interaction, that building up of one another, which, as previously noted may be even more formative than the faculty-student interaction; (f) Student–Content interaction, which involves the student's direct processing of the information; and (g) Student–Self interaction, which involves the life-changing deliberation and decision-making that occurs in the student's thoughts, values, and actions.

Evaluation. Whether online or offline, principles of evaluation remain basically the same. *Formative* evaluation, or *assessment,* is used to identify weaknesses in learning and teaching, not to grade performance. *Summative* evaluation (or simply, *evaluation*) measures student performance against objectives established by the instructor.

Examples of formative assessment could be daily or weekly quizzes, brief written self-evaluations, or a journal with reflections on class content to be regularly read by the instructor. Formative feedback is greatly enhanced by the technology, allowing the instructor or group members to give very quick yet thoughtful feedback.

Summative evaluations might include an exam, an essay, an individual or group project, or an electronic portfolio. A must for any summative evaluation is the use of rubrics, which lay out the student performance criteria in great detail. If used from the beginning of a course to the end, rubrics provide a guide to learning, as well as to formative and summative evaluation (Rocco, 2007).

CONCLUSION

Whether online or offline, distance or face-to-face, the educational process looks like this: *Utilizing instructor and student input, the teacher is guided and empowered by God to devise and employ a learning space where the learning community can be led in actively and reflectively engaging with the curriculum for the purpose of bringing about lasting, truth-based, and holistically assessed change in the learners.* Taking this process into the strange world of online learning requires adjustments. We assume that online learning is an important development that must be responded to in a thoroughly Christian and educationally sound way. Current theorizing about distance education, in our opinion, does not really take us into new understandings of the nature of teaching and learning. However, the rise of these new modes of educational delivery have happily forced all of us in education to revisit important questions like "How do people learn anything?" and "How can we help them do this?"

In the end, the primary task of online educators is to creatively adapt what we already know about good education to the new, virtual learning space. For Christian educators, this requires dependence on the Holy Spirit and hard work organizing the various components of the teaching-learning process to the best advantage of the virtual student.

REFERENCES

Bain, K. (2004). *What the best college teachers do.* Cambridge, MA: Harvard University Press.

Baviskar, S. N., Hartle, R. T., & Whitney, T. (2009). Essential criteria to characterize constructivist teaching: Derived from a review of the literature and applied to five constructivist-teaching method articles. *International Journal of Science Education, 31*(4), 541–550.

Bell, F. (2011). Connectivism: Its place in theory-informed research and innovation in technology-enabled learning. *International Review of Research in Open and Distance Learning, 12*(3), 98–118.

Bernard, R. M., Abrami, P. C., Lou, Y., Borokhovsk, E., Wade, A., Wosney, L., et al. (2004). How does distance education compare with classroom instruction? A meta-analysis of the empirical literature. *Review of Educational Research, 74*(3), 379–439.

Bloom, B. S. (Ed.). (1956). *Taxonomy of educational objectives: Handbook 1: Cognitive domain.* New York: David McKay.

Brown, R. E. (2001). The process of community-building in distance learning classes. *Journal of Asynchronous Learning Networks 5*(2). [On-line journal]. Accessed September 28, 2001. Available: http://www.aln.org/alnweb/journal/Vol5 issue2/Brown/Brown.htm

Burgess, H. W. (1996). *Models of religious education: Theory and practice in historical contemporary perspective.* Grand Rapids, MI: Baker Books House.

Churches, A. (2008). Bloom's digital taxonomy. *Educational Origami.* Retrieved June 20, 2011, from edorigami.wikispaces.com/Bloom%27s+Digital+Taxonomy

de Tocqueville, A. (1966). *Democracy in America: Vol. 1.* H. Reeve (Trans.). New Rochelle, NY: Arlington House. (Original work published 1835)

Downs, P. G. (1994). *Teaching for spiritual growth: An introduction to Christian education.* Grand Rapids: Eerdmans.

Giossos, Y., Koutsouba, M., Lionarakis, A., & Skavantzos, K. (2009). Reconsidering Moore's transactional distance theory. *European Journal of Open, Distance and E-Learning,* (2). Retrieved August 1, 2011 from www.eurodl.org/?article=374

Haythornthwaite, C., Kazmer, M. M., Robins, J., & Shoemaker, S. (2000). Community development among distance learners: Temporal and technological dimensions. *Journal of Computer-Mediated Communication, 6*(1). Retrieved June 20, 2011 from http://www.ascusc.org/jcmc/vol6/issue1/haythornthwaite.html

Heinemann, M. H. (2007). Teacher-student interaction and learning in on-line theological education, Part IV: Findings and conclusions. *Christian Higher Education, 6*(3), 185–206.

Illich, I. (1970). *Deschooling society.* New York: Harper & Row.

Kop, R., & Hill, A. (2008). Connectivism: Learning theory of the future or vestige of the past? *International Review of Research in Open and Distance Learning, 9*(3), 1–13.

Liu, C. H., & Matthews, R. (2005). Vygotsky's philosophy: Constructivism and its criticisms examined. *International Education Journal, 6*(3), 386–399.

Lowman, J. (1985). *Mastering the techniques of teaching.* San Francisco, CA: Jossey-Bass.

Moore, M. G., & Kearsley, G. (2011). *Distance education: A systems view of online learning* (3rd ed.). Belmont, CA: Wadsworth.

McLuhan, M. (1964). *Understanding media.* Cambridge, MA: MIT Press.

Palloff, R. M., & Pratt, K. (2003). *The virtual student: A profile and guide to working with online learners.* San Francisco: Jossey-Bass.

Phillips, D. C. (1995) The good, the bad, and the ugly: The many faces of constructivism. *Educational Researcher, 24*(7), 5–12.

Prensky, M. (2001). Digital natives, digital immigrants. *On the Horizon, 9*(5), 1–6. Retrieved from http://www.marcprensky.com/writing/Prensky%20-%20Digital%20Natives,%20Digital%20Immigrants%20-%20Part1.pdf

Rocco, S. (2007). Online assessment and evaluation. In S. C. O. Conceição (Ed.), *Teaching strategies in the online environment* (pp. 75–86). San Francisco: Jossey-Bass.

Wolcott, L. L. (1995). The distance teacher as reflective practitioner. *Educational Technology, 35*(1), 39–43.

CHAPTER 2

ADULT LEARNING THEORY AND ONLINE LEARNING

Stephen D. Lowe
Erskine Theological Seminary

The participation of adult learners in various forms of distance education is not a recent development. Seevers (1993) and White (2006) note that the Apostle Paul involved Christian adult believers in the earliest form of Christian distance education when he employed the epistle as a form of mediated instruction that helped bridge the gap that separated teacher (Paul) from students (Christians in various parts of the Roman Empire in the first century).

Grattan (1971) reminds us "there is no possibility of understanding adult education historically without a clear comprehension of the religious motivation for its promotion" (p. 48). This is even truer concerning the development of correspondence education in the United States. In 1873, Rev. John Vincent, who would later (1888) become a bishop in the Methodist Church, established the earliest form of progressive and systematic correspondence study (Knowles, 1977). In fact, William Rainey Harper, then professor of Hebrew at Yale, created the first correspondence courses offered through Vincent's Chautauqua Institute in 1879 (Grattan, 1955). Harper and others offered courses in Greek, Latin, and biblical Hebrew through

Best Practices of Online Education, pages 17–30
Copyright © 2012 by Information Age Publishing
All rights of reproduction in any form reserved.

correspondence. Later Harper went on to become the founding president of the University of Chicago in 1892 and launched the first university-based correspondence program in the United States. Harper's student at Yale, R.A. Torrey, helped D.L. Moody create adult Bible correspondence study at Moody Bible Institute of Chicago beginning in 1901. Getz (1986) speculates that Harper influenced Torrey in his thinking about extension or correspondence education.

Today in the United States and around the world, the vast majority of those studying at a distance online and through a variety of mediated forms of instruction are adults. The most recent Sloan Consortium statistics (Staying the Course—Online Education in the United States, 2008) indicate that almost four million adult students are studying online in our colleges and universities. In spite of the vast numbers of adults learning online, very little of online instruction design and delivery takes adult learning characteristics into consideration. Ignoring the learning needs, characteristics, and orientations of the primary student population seems quite uncharacteristic of thoughtful educators. One possible reason for this oversight may be educator fascination with the technology used to deliver the educational experience (Levine, 2005). Another possible reason is a false assumption that we already know our learners and, therefore, do not need to think critically about designing and delivering online education specifically for them. Still a third possible reason for this reality is that most educators working in online education know little about the unique learning characteristics, needs, and orientations of adult learners. A final possible reason for the present situation is a combination of all of the above, complicated by other unknown factors yet to be determined. However, if we wish to maximize the impact of our online learning opportunities for adult students, we must appreciate the unique learner profile of our adult students to design and deliver our online courses accordingly.

DEFINING ADULTHOOD

Before we can explore how we incorporate adult learning principles into online adult learning, we must define exactly what we mean by an adult. When defining adulthood we must consider not only age and developmental characteristics but also social roles most often associated with adulthood. Neugarten (1996) summarizes the complex variables at work in defining the parameters of adulthood when she writes, "In modern America people are considered adults in the political system when they reach 18 and are given the right to vote; but they are not adults in the family system until they marry and take on the responsibilities of parenthood. Or people may be adult in the family system, but if they are still in school they are not yet adults in the economic system" (p. 72). Age norms and age expectations of a given society affect whether or not an adult is "on time," "early," or "late" within the systems mentioned by Neugarten (1996). The cultural and personal awareness of timing across the so-called "developmental tasks" of adulthood changes over time in any given society (Havighurst, 1972).

Developmental life span characteristics that incorporate all of the variables and others referenced by Neugarten allow the interested observer to posit clearly demarcated phases agreed upon by most adult development theorists (Stevens-Long & Commons, 1992). Havighurst (1972) and Neugarten (1974) offer the following adult life span divisions:

- 19–35
- Early adulthood 36–60
- Middle adulthood 61+
- Later adulthood

Probably the most critical ingredient for defining an adult is the psychological dimension of adulthood (Knowles, 1980). According to Knowles, "psychologically, we become adults when we arrive at a self-concept of being responsible for our own lives, of being self-directing" (1980, p. 64). The awareness of being self-directed and interdependent marks a change in self-perception that finds being other-directed and other-dependent no longer satisfying. The movement from a pedagogical psychology to an andragogical psychology is a difficult transition to traverse for most adults. The reason is that there are few opportunities during the dependent stage of the lifespan to practice the skills needed to become more self-directed and independent. The Apostle Paul actually used the language of pedagogy in his Epistle to the Galatians when describing our Christian status as dependent children during the period of Law in redemptive history. He said that God's people were like children "under guardians and managers until the date set by the father" (Gal. 4:2, New American Standard Version). In this respect, Paul writes, "the law has become our tutor to lead us to Christ" (Gal. 3:24). The English word "tutor" is the Greek word *paidagogos* from which we derive our educational term "pedagogy." Most adults experience difficulty transitioning from having someone telling them what to do, when to do it, and how to do it, to making all those determinations for themselves. Some adults embrace the freedom such a change brings, while others struggle with it because they like the security and comfort of having others in charge. In the Pauline communities the legalists preferred to make decisions of faith for others and keep them permanently dependent, while the Apostle Paul called his converts to a newfound freedom in Christ that embraced their spiritual adulthood (Gal. 5:1; Eph. 4:13). The competing self-perceptions I've described manifest themselves in adult cognitive style making one either "syllabus bound" (convergent thinking leading to one right answer) or "syllabus free" (divergent thinking leading to many acceptable answers) (Lovell, 1980).

Online Christian education as typically practiced in the United States assumes a mature adult psychology in the design and structure of courses regarding learner expectations but often without necessarily being fully informed and aware of the theories and models supporting such practice. While those doing online education at public institutions have started to address this issue, those of us serving in online Christian education have more work to do to catch up. This chapter will advocate for the necessity of studying adult education theories, principles, and practices for the express purpose of being more fully informed and aware of how best to design and structure online Christian education learning experiences for adult learners. Since most forms of online Christian higher education involve those who either are on the threshold of adulthood or fully imbedded in it, it is incumbent upon us to understand our students as adult learners.

ANDRAGOGICAL ASSUMPTIONS

The study of adults as a unique learner species originated in the United States with the publication of Eduard C. Lindeman's *The Meaning of Adult Education* (1926). He worked during his early career in the National Youth Administration in Massachusetts, and it was there that he influenced the thought of another major contributor to adult learning theory, Malcolm Knowles. Malcolm considered Lindeman his professional mentor, and one detects Lindeman's influence in many of Knowles' subsequent publications, especially his first published work *Informal Adult Education* (1950). It was his experiences as an adult educator in organizations like the National Youth Association and the YMCA, along with the influence of Eduard Lindeman, that informed many of the precepts outlined in Knowles' original publication. In particular, Knowles came to appreciate the powerful influence of social interaction among adult participants in learning communities. Lindeman encouraged Knowles to further his education and recommended the University of Chicago where he came under the influence of his academic advisor Cyril Houle, whose work on adult learning orientations greatly influenced the field of adult education. Houle's concept of adult learner orientations, published in *The Inquiring Mind* (1961), further refined Knowles' understanding of the role of social interaction in adult learning settings. Houle conceptualized adult learner orientations as a powerful interaction between internal and external influences and motivations. In 1959, Knowles joined the faculty of Boston University as Associate Professor of Adult Education. In this position he published three of his most influential works, cementing his credentials as the father of American adult education: *The Modern Practice of Adult Education: Pedagogy versus Andragogy* (1970); *The Adult Learner* (1973); and *Self-Directed Learning* (1975). What emerged from this publishing output was a term forever associated with Knowles, although he did not coin it: *andragogy*. He defined the term as "the art and science of helping adults learn." Although originally he had hoped that this concept would emerge into a full-blown theory of adult learning, later he described it as *a set of assumptions* that comprised a model of adult learning. He initially thought of adult education (andragogy) as entirely different from child education (pedagogy), but this too he later modified and considered the two as polar opposites on a continuum that could move either direction depending upon learning outcomes (Knowles, 1980).

These two examples illustrate one of the greatest strengths of Knowles as an educator: his ability to analyze his own work in light of the assessment of educational colleagues. In other words, Knowles actually practiced what he preached! He believed that adult learners come to understanding and developmental growth because of their interaction with knowledge, other learners, and their own unique yet educationally valid experiences. His interactions with other colleagues modified his understanding of his own adult learning concepts. His modified views in turn influenced his colleagues in their own thinking and thus the process unfolded across his academic career. When I met him in 1991 at the age of 78, he was still open to the views of others (including a still wet behind the ears newly minted Ph.D. in adult education) and offered his views on adult learning tentatively. Such humility about what we know and think about adult learning, from the undisputed leader of the field during his lifetime, will mark the descriptions and recommendations that follow. The Apostle Paul said of our Christian understanding of love that, "we know in part" and "we see in a mirror dimly" (1 Cor. 13:9, 12). What the Apostle said about love one may say about many things, including how one understands adult learning. It is impossible to summarize what we know about a species of learner when there is so much diversity present in the population. All of our generalizations are crude descriptors that apply to some but not to all. At the same time, we cannot conceive of adult learners as a scientific object of study divorced from the social situations, contexts, and settings in which they live and study. An ecological perspective keeps us from a laboratory bias that distorts the subject because we are studying it in an artificial environment.

While the concept of andragogy that Knowles advocated continues "in sparking debate" (Cross, 1981, p. 228) among adult educators (Brookfield, 1986; Burge, 1988; Elias, 1979; Houle, 1972; Pratt, 1984; Sandlin, 2005), the fact that it continues to prod discussion indicates that its explanatory power is still a viable option that must be considered seriously (Merriam, 2001). While fully aware of its limitations as a theory of adult learning, nonetheless, I think it offers a valid starting point for those new to the concept of adult learning theory. Concomitant with Knowles' concept of andragogy is his concept of self-directed learning, both of which Merriam observes still have "staying power" (2001, p. 3) as explanatory models of adult learning, especially within the context of online Christian education. While applauding much that Knowles propounded about designing and facilitating adult learning, we must also offer caution, especially concerning the uncritical assumptions about American individualism. I will offer my own ecological perspective as a viable context within which to imbed the concept of andragogy and self-direction.

Salient Andragogical Principles and Online Christian Education

While Knowles certainly identified the set of assumptions that guided his understanding of adult learning (1970, 1973), I prefer the excellent summary of those assumptions provided by Merriam (2001). She argues that the andragogical perspective assumes an adult learner who: (a) has an independent self-concept and who can direct his or her own learning, (b) has accumulated a reservoir of life experiences that is a rich resource for learning, (c) has learning needs closely related to changing social roles, (d) is problem-centered and interested in immediate application of knowledge, and (e) is motivated to learn by internal rather than external factors. How can these five andragogical assumptions positively influence the design and practice of online Christian education?

Assumption #1—It often baffles me by how educators treat adults and likewise how adults allow educators to treat them. Although adults enter our online courses having proven their ability to make educational decisions about their own learning (otherwise they would not be there!), we treat them as if they have just hopped off the educational boat and know nothing about how to learn. These same adults manage their own financial affairs, business interests, political concerns, and family responsibilities. Even college age adults now have their own credit cards, financial accounts, loan contracts, and can navigate the complicated labyrinth of contemporary higher education. However, when they enter our world of online education we treat them as if none of those abilities to make decisions and manage their own lives has any connection to what and how we want to teach them. Knowles had a higher opinion of adults than many of us who teach adults. It was not, however, an ivory tower optimism. Knowles would have accepted the wisdom of Vygotsky's (1978) concept of educational scaffolding that provided academic and relational support at the outset with the intention of gradually dismantling it as the adult matured in his/her ability to function in the educational setting. Lowe (2005) proposed the Providing Academic and Relational Support (PARS) model for distance education, incorporating elements of Knowles and Vygotsky into a practical framework that looks realistically at the developmental capacity of adult learners. The PARS model does not assume that adults arrive in full bloom regarding self-concept and ability to take responsibility for their own learning. Some adults may in fact resist such expectations because previous educational experiences have conditioned them to be passive, dependent, and to repress their adult capacities.

One of the best ways to address the issue posed by Assumption #1 in online Christian education is by providing a general introductory course or orientation experience for online students. Many institutions offer some kind of introductory or orientation experience, but most of the time it addresses technical matters rather than an orientation to learning online for adults. Gibson (1996) made the observation regarding online instruction that "a student orientation that introduces procedures for learning at a distance . . . and instruction in the process of directing one's own learning and in study strategies also seems appropriate early in a student's program" (pp. 32–33).

Assumption #2—Capitalizing on the rich life and learning experiences of adult students in online education means, as Christians, honoring the way in which God has worked in students' lives to bring them to our courses or our institutions. If we truly believe that "all things work together for good" (Rom. 8:28) and that God prepares his people "for a time such as this" (Esther 4:14), then we must also believe that God prepares our students to receive our instruction through their many experiences. The role of student experience marks a significant difference between treating students as children rather than as adults. Children have little in the way of accumulated experience and derived wisdom to draw upon, but adults bring a vast reservoir of experience to bear on new learning experiences. Educators have explored the potential role that experience plays in the learning process (Dewey, 1938; Kolb, 1984). Most recently Pierre F. Dominicé (2000), professor of adult education at the University of Geneva, has proposed the use of educational biography with adult learners that allows them "to prepare and share life histories that become vehicles through which these learners can reflect on their educational experiences" and that allows adult students to "deepen their understanding of their own ways of learning and of their existing knowledge" (p. xv). Dominicé's approach to educational biography for adult learners calls for the adult to self-analyze what he calls the *adult relation to knowledge.* He proposes three possible sources of knowledge: science, tradition, and conviction. As Christian educators, we might add a fourth: revelation. The narratives that adult learners create ask them to consider their experiences through these four lenses, which create in effect "a frame of reference, a way of thinking, a cohesiveness that can be understood as a type of structure of interpretation" (Dominicé, 2000, p. 102). One could also ask that students add a fifth source of knowledge, which is the immediate field or discipline represented by the course or cluster of courses that a student would take. For instance, someone teaching an Old Testament survey class online might ask adult students to reflect upon what they have learned about the Old Testament as a discipline through Bible studies, Sunday School classes, sermons, workshops, or personal study. The educational biography based in experience allows both the adult student and the teacher of adults to have a rich experiential platform upon which to begin study together.

Assumption #3—The social and professional roles that adults assume impact their learning in a variety of ways that need to be reflected in how we design and practice online Christian education. Roles influence an adults' orientation to learning and their readiness to learn. Generally, social roles make adult learners more pragmatic, goal-oriented, and needing to see the immediacy of knowledge applied to their social and professional roles. Since adults tend to be goal oriented (Houle, 1961), online courses need to be clear and unambiguous about course objectives. Since adults like to know why they need to learn something, specifying relevancy to potential work environments or fields of study will eliminate any potential dissonance. Allowing for multiple ways of applying or using information provided in a course instead of locking students into one teacher-preferred approach makes allowance for this assumption regarding adult learning. For instance, an online course in Christian education might ask students to apply specific principles in preaching, administrating, teaching, or in a variety of settings such as Bible studies, Sunday School classes, workshops, seminars, congregational worship, higher education classroom, and so on.

Assumption #4—Problem-centered learning with immediate application to professional or ministry settings seems ideally suited to online Christian learning. Knowles (1972) made it clear that "the adult... comes into an educational activity largely because he/she is experiencing some inadequacy in coping with current life problems. He/she wants to apply tomorrow what he/she learns today, so his/her time perspective is one of immediacy of application" (p. 36). For many years, other adult educators have advocated the use of problem-posing (Freire, 1970), problem-solving (Mezirow, 1991), or problem-based (Wilkerson & Gijselaers, 1996) learning as a centerpiece of adult learning theory. Mezirow asserts that, "problem solving is central" (p. 94) to his notion of transformative adult learning. Allen Tough's (1971) famous research at the University of Toronto concluded by noting, "most adult learning begins because of a problem" (p. 72).

Online learning involving adult learners that is sensitive to this problem-oriented perspective will seek to incorporate this motivational orientation into the structured requirements of a course. Immediacy of application of concepts learned means that online instructors capitalize on the problem-centered orientation of adult learners but go beyond that. An online instructor may go beyond the initial motivation adults bring to online learning by providing multiple avenues for application built into course requirements. Leaving any subject purely at the theoretical level with adult learners invites disinterest and possible rejection of the validity of the theoretical concepts. Usefulness of information in practical contexts and settings is a number one concern of adult learners. Online instructors who fail to include practical application in their online classes will have difficulty retaining adult learners who are deeply motivated by this concern.

Assumption #5—Adult learners have a deep internal motivation to learn that instructors must respect in any online adult learning context. Wlod-kowski (2008) analogizes intrinsic motivation to "a cork rising through water," which surfaces in any learning context "because the environment elicits it" (p. 7). All adult learners have an innate curiosity that intrinsically motivates them to learn, but this basic predisposition needs nurturing and encouragement by the learning environment. Intrinsic motivation derives from internalized attitudes that to some extent reflect cultural influences. Adults are motivated to learn for three different reasons: (a) because they *have to*; (b) because they *ought to*; or (c) because they *want to*. Some adults learn because someone compels them to learn for job-related or other reasons. Other adults learn for externally oriented reasons imposed by society or family. Finally, most adults learn because of a deep desire to master their world and understand it fully. Online learning experiences that honor the intrinsic motivational capacity of adult learners will seek to nurture it, not stifle it. In practice, this means linking motivational baggage checked upon arrival in an online course with instructional needs to cover a spectrum of knowledge in order to achieve a certain level of subject-matter mastery.

ADVANCES IN ADULT LEARNING THEORY SINCE KNOWLES

While the concept of andragogy developed by Knowles held sway in the first two decades after its publication, interest in it as a viable theory or model of adult learning has waned. In its place, proposals that are more expansive have captured the interest and imagination of those who work with adult learners. In particular, transformative learning theories proposed by Friere (1970) and Mezirow (1991) and situated or contextualized theories proposed by Lave and Wenger (1998) dominate research publications.

The beneficial perspectives offered by these additions to the discussion on adult learning theory mitigate limitations and weaknesses of andragogy.

Transformative models broaden one's perspective to include internal processes of human development engendered by learning experiences. Contextualized or situated models of adult learning liberate adult learners and practitioners from the individualistic limitations of andragogy and its philosophical underpinnings in humanistic psychology.

The contextualized or situated models of adult learning find agreement with those who offer a transactive or interactive view of human development (Bronfenbrenner, 1979; Lerner, 2002; Magnusson & Allen, 1983). Reciprocity, which involves "concomitant mutual feedback" (Bronfenbrenner, 1979, p. 57) between two or more persons creates "bidirectional interaction between an individual and his or her environment" (Magnusson & Allen, 1983, p. 7). The bidirectional interaction creates a reciprocal relationship that makes possible environmental influences upon persons, as well as a person-to-person impact. Such dynamic social bi-directionality understands the developing person as an active agent in his/her own development acting with intentionality and purpose. Consequently, one cannot explain or understand individual functioning and development apart from this "environmental context in which the individual develops and is functioning" (Magnusson & Allen, 1983, p. 8). Social relationships in the microsystem and larger social ecology make it possible for persons to be "interconnected in a dynamic process of mutual influence and change" (Magnusson & Allen, 1983, p. 8).

Such multi-level social interactions take place across the lifespan and make possible "the course of individual development" (Lerner, 2002, p. 165). Further, these developmentally instigative interactions operate holistically upon the developing person. Aspects of this holistic development include biological, psychological, behavioral, and mental components that interact within the personal ecosystem to bring about whole person development. As a result, the whole person is the center of such a "holistic interactionist viewpoint" (Lerner, 2002, p. 176). Magnusson, Lerner, and Bronfenbrenner would argue that any analysis of the developing person that only takes into account a single aspect of this whole person necessarily produces an incomplete picture of that person. At the same time, "A change in one aspect affects related parts of the subsystem and, sometimes, the whole organism" (Magnusson & Stattin, 1998, p. 700). Magnusson (1999a, 1999b) and Magnusson and Stattin (1998) broaden out Bronfenbrenner's concept of reciprocity beyond the self-contained dyadic relationship in the microsystem as a major feature of interactional developmental dynamics. Thus, these developmentally beneficial social interactions serve as influences on human development across the lifespan. All social networks partake of this interactive-reciprocal quality and produce changes in behavior, attitudes, emotions, beliefs, knowledge, and values among all participating persons producing positive human development and adaptation.

This contextualized, situated, and ecological understanding of adult learning recognizes that learning is not just an individually transformative experience (Mezirow, 1991) but also a socially interactive experience that "instigates" (Bronfenbrenner, 2005) further development and transformation—not just individual development and transformation but "reciprocal development" of all the persons involved in the learning experience. The reciprocal exchanges between persons that take various forms and degrees of interaction serve as what Bronfenbrenner (2005) describes as "developmentally instigative activities" (p. 10). This leads Bronfenbrenner to Proposition C: "If one member of a dyad undergoes developmental change, the other is also likely to do so" (p. 65). Bronfenbrenner refers to this phenomenon "as a context not merely of reciprocal interaction but of reciprocal development" (p. 65). Thus reciprocal interaction leads to reciprocal development. The developmental system that is created by these relationships becomes a "vehicle...that stimulates and sustains development processes...as long as they remain interconnected...in a bond" (p. 66).

Situated contexts where learners meet are "communities of practice" (Wenger, 1999), which engender a shared approach to meaning making, understanding, apprehension, and cognitive functioning. Thus a level of cognitive mastery or "situated cognition" (Merriam, 2004) emerges, which is shared among the members of the situated learning community. The context or situation in which such developmentally beneficial transactions occur may be quite varied. As Merriam (2004) indicates, "the place in which situated cognition occurs is the community of practice, which might be a family, a classroom, a workplace, an online community, a town, or a corporation" (p. 211). These types of learning communities, as Merriam suggests, do not require face-to-face encounters but may emerge in any context where various types of interactions and transactions occur between learners. Collective cognition does not require persons to occupy collective space simultaneously.

Online courses in Christian higher education provide Christian institutions an opportunity to create a networked learning community of adults that recognizes students as situated in specific familial and church contexts that instructors need to integrate into online learning experiences (Kemp, 2010). Spider web-like social connections and relationships reflected in our online learning communities among learners and between learners and their own social networks highlight the ecological nature of human social networks and their impact on adult learning. Ivan Illich's (1970) concept of "learning webs" helps us understand the power of creating interconnections between and among learners and their social contexts. If we are going to move online Christian education to the next level of development and impact, then we must embrace the situated, contextualized, and ecological reality of life and learning in order to maximize our learning capacity and our potential for greater transformation into the image of Christ. It will help us recognize that our educational efforts will not just impact the students who enroll in our courses and degree programs but will spill over into the multitude of social networks that our students inhabit. It is this reality that prompted Barabasi (2003) to note, "the Apostle Paul's message reached people he never met" (p. 19). Indeed, our messages will also reach people we have never met, and we will reach people who never enrolled in our courses. Such is the power of situated social ecologies. We all experience intricately interconnected relationships with one another for good or for ill, and the sooner we honor and appreciate this human social reality and the spiritual reality inhabited in the Body of Christ, the more effective, transformative, and far-reaching our online adult learning communities will be.

REFERENCES

Barabasi, A. L. (2003). *Linked: How everything is connected to everything else and what it means for business, science, and everyday life.* London: Penguin Books.

Bronfenbrenner, U. (1979). *The ecology of human development.* Cambridge: Harvard University Press.

Bronfenbrenner, U. (2005). *Making human beings human.* Thousand Oaks, CA: Sage.

Brookfield, S. D. (1986). *Understanding and facilitating adult learning.* San Francisco: Jossey-Bass.

Burge, L. (1988). Beyond andragogy: Some explorations for distance learning design. *Journal of Distance Education, 3*(1), 5–23.

Cross, P. K. (1981). *Adults as learners.* San Francisco: Jossey-Bass.

Dewey, J. (1938). *Experience and education.* New York: Macmillan.

Dominicé, P. (2000). *Learning from our lives.* San Francisco: Jossey-Bass.

Elias, J. L. (1979). Andragogy revisited. *Adult Education, 29*(4), 252–256.

Freire, P. (1970). *Pedagogy of the oppressed.* New York: Continuum Books.

Getz, G. A. (1986). *MBI: The story of Moody Bible Institute.* Chicago: Moody Press.

Gibson, C. C. (1996). Toward an understanding of academic self-concept in distance education. *The American Journal of Distance Education, 10*(1), 23–36.

Grattan, C. H. (1955). *In quest of knowledge: A historical perspective on adult education.* New York: Association Press.

Grattan, C. H. (1971). *American ideas about adult education 1710–1951.* New York: Bureau of Publications, Teachers College.

Havighurst, R. (1972). *Developmental tasks and education.* New York: David McKay Company, Inc.

Houle, C. O. (1961). *The inquiring mind.* Madison, WI: The University of Wisconsin Press.

Houle, C. O. (1972). *The design of education.* San Francisco: Jossey-Bass.

Illich, I. (1970). *Deschooling society.* New York: Harper and Row.

Kemp, S. (2010). Situated learning: Optimizing experiential learning through God-given learning community. *Christian Education Journal, Series 3, 7*(1), 118–143.

Knowles, M. S. (1950). *Informal adult education.* New York: Association Press.

Knowles, M. S. (1970). *The modern practice of adult education: Andragogy versus pedagogy*. New York: Association Press.

Knowles, M. S. (1972). Innovations in teaching styles and approaches based upon adult learning. *Journal of Education for Social Work, 8*(2), 32–39.

Knowles, M. S. (1973). *The adult learner: A neglected species*. Houston, TX: Gulf Publishing Company.

Knowles, M. S. (1975). Self-*directed learning*. Cambridge, MA: Cambridge Adult Education.

Knowles, M. S. (1977). *The adult education movement in the United States*. Malabar, FL: Krieger Publishing.

Knowles, M. S. (1980). *The modern practice of adult education: From pedagogy to andragogy*. New York: Association Press.

Kolb, D. (1984). *Experiential learning: Experience as the source of learning and development*. Englewood Cliffs, NJ: Prentice Hall.

Lave, J., & Wenger, E. (1998). *Communities of practice: Learning, meaning, and identity*. Cambridge, MA: University Press.

Lerner, R. M. (2002). *Concepts and theories of human development*. Mahwah, NJ: Lawrence Erlbaum Associates.

Levine, S. J. (2005). *Making distance education work: Understanding learning and learners at a distance*. Okemos, MI: LearnerAssociates.net.

Lindeman, E. C. (1926). *The meaning of adult education*. New York: New Republic.

Lovell, R. B. (1980). *Adult learning*. London: Croom Helm.

Lowe, S. D. (2005). Responding to learner needs in distance education: Providing academic and relational support (PARS). In S. J. Levine (Ed.), *Making distance education work: Understanding learning and learners at a distance*. Okemos, MI: LearnerAssociates.net.

Magnusson, D. (1999a). Holistic interactionism: A perspective for research on personality development. In L. Pervin & O. John (Eds.), *Handbook of personality: Theory and research* (2nd ed., pp. 219–247). New York: Guilfod Press.

Magnusson, D. (1999b). On the individual: A person-oriented approach to developmental research. *European Psychologist, 4*(4), 205–218.

Magnusson, D. & Allen, V. L. (1983). *Human development: An interactional perspective*. New York: McGraw Hill.

Magnusson, D. & Stattin, H. (1998). Person-context interaction theories. In R. Lerner (Ed.), *Handbook of child psychology, Vol. I: Theoretical models of human development*. New York: Wiley and Sons.

Merriam, S. (2001). Andragogy and self-directed learning: Pillars of adult learning theory. In S. Merriam (Ed.), *The new update on adult learning theory, No. 89* (pp. 3–14). San Francisco: Jossey-Bass.

Merriam, S. (2004). The changing landscape of adult learning theory. In J. Comings, B. Garner, & C. Smith (Eds.), *Review of adult learning and literacy: Connecting research, policy, and practice* (pp. 199–220). Mahwah, NJ: Lawrence Erlbaum Associates.

Mezirow, J. (1991). *Transformative dimensions of adult learning*. San Francisco: Jossey-Bass.

Neugarten, B. L. (1974). Age groups in American society and the rise of the young old. *Annals of American Academy of Science, 14*(1), 187–198.

Neugarten, B. L. (1996). *The meanings of age.* Chicago: The University of Chicago Press.

Pratt, D. D. (1984). Andragogical assumptions: Some counter-intuitive logic. *Proceedings of the Adult Education Research Conference,* (pp. 147–153). Raleigh, NC: North Carolina State University.

Sandlin, J. A. (2005). Andragogy and its discontents: An analysis of andragogy from three critical perspectives. *PAACE Journal of Lifelong Learning, 14,* 25–42.

Seevers, G. L., Jr. (1993). *Identification of criteria for delivery of theological education through distance education: An interdisciplinary Delphi study.* Unpublished doctoral dissertation. Virginia Polytechnic Institute and State University, Blacksburg, VA.

Stevens-Long, J., & Commons, M.L. (1992). *Adult life: Developmental Processes.* Mountain View, CA: Mayfield Publishing Company.

Tough, A. (1971). *The adult's learning projects.* Toronto: OISE.

Vygotsky, L. S. (1978). *Mind in society: The development of higher psychological processes.* Cambridge, MA: Harvard University Press.

Wenger, E. (1999). *Communities of practice: Learning, meaning, and identity.* Cambridge, MA: University Press.

White, R. (2006). Promoting spiritual formation in distance education. *Christian Education Journal, 3*(2), 303–315.

Wilkerson, L., & Gijselaers, W. H. (1996). *Bringing problem-based learning to higher education: Theory and practice, No. 68.* San Francisco: Jossey-Bass.

Wlodkowski, R. J. (2008). *Enhancing adult motivation to learn: A comprehensive guide for teaching all adults.* San Francisco: Jossey-Bass.

CHAPTER 3

DEVELOPING ONLINE LEARNING COMMUNITIES

Mark A. Maddix
Northwest Nazarene University

Most educators would agree that learning and growth takes places best through social interaction in a communal setting. Historically communal learning activities took place in a traditional classroom context; however, with the advent of technology that is no longer the case. While learning communities have been considered to be bound to a traditional classroom (Palloff & Pratt, 1999), the growth of social networking such as Facebook, Twitter, blogging, and online courses have demonstrated how communities can transcend physical space and still have actively engaged learners (Vesely, Bloom, & Sherlock, 2007). These growing virtual learning communities are a testimony to the way social interaction and relationships are developed online. In 2009, more than one in four students in higher education took at least one course online (Allen & Seaman, 2010). There is a growing acceptance that educating students beyond the traditional classroom is a major element in the university or seminary mission. In 2009 over 2,500 colleges and universities offered online courses (Allen & Seaman, 2010), which includes Christian colleges, universities, and seminaries. Since online courses and programs are changing the landscape of education in

Best Practices of Online Education, pages 31–40
Copyright © 2012 by Information Age Publishing

31

general and Christian higher education in particular, the development of learning communities in online courses is essential to effective learning and formation.

DEFINING LEARNING COMMUNITIES

The concept of learning communities has been discussed for more than two decades. Research has clearly shown that functioning in a learning community can enhance the learning that occurs among members. Pam Vesely et al. (2007) indicate that while communities have been defined in a variety of different ways, these elements of community are frequently identified:

1. A sense of shared purpose,
2. The establishment of boundaries defining who is a member and who is not,
3. The establishment and enforcement of rules/policies regarding community behavior,
4. Interaction among members (both faculty and students), and
5. A level of trust, respect and support among community members.

Learning communities that foster these elements help individual learners "achieve what they cannot on their own" (Shea, Sau Li, & Pickett, 2006, p. 155). They create a context that provides opportunities for dialogue and engagement that allows students to collaborate in learning. This sharing occurs through interaction within social networks that are formed in the community. This is best expressed in the root word for community, *communicare*, which means "to share" (Palloff & Pratt, 1999, p. 25).

Online learning courses, built on student and faculty interaction, have proven to provide effective learning (Palloff & Pratt, 2007). These learning communities are developing significant relationships with peers, faculty, and with God. Studies indicate that learning and growth does take place in online learning communities (Palloff & Pratt, 2007). The primary goal in online courses is the creation of communities of learners, where the learner finds opportunities to be leader and teacher. Traditional face to face courses do not guarantee community any more than distance learning courses (Cannell, 1999). Many students drive to campus to take classes, sit in the back row, and do not engage their colleagues or professor in the learning process. In online learning communities each student is active in online interaction and dialogue. In essence everyone is in the front row. Also, online courses that foster learning communities provide an opportunity for people to share life together. When interactions among students and faculty are directed toward the purpose for which the community was formed, it is considered collaboration. Collaborative learning has shown to be very important in the development of learning communities and in achievement of the desired outcomes for a course (Palloff & Pratt, 1999).

WHY ONLINE LEARNING COMMUNITIES?

Given the growth of online courses in institutions of Christian higher education, there is an increased interest in online learning communities and their impact on education. One of the reasons for the interest in online learning communities has been to better understand and address the dropout rates among distance education students. Studies show that the dropout rates are 10 to 20% higher in online courses than in traditional courses (Carr, 2000). Many students drop out due to issues of isolation and disconnection from the professor and students in the course. Student dropout impacts the quality of education and the financial viability of these courses. The development of online learning communities reduces this feeling of isolation and separation and student dropouts.

Another reason Christian higher educational institutions are concerned about developing learning communities concerns how students are being formed and shaped as persons of faith. With the removal of personal interaction in the online course, there is greater concern that students are not being modeled Christian values and beliefs. The formative role of online education has been one of the primary avenues of criticism in Christian colleges, universities, and seminaries. The research testifies that effective learning can take place in online course (United States Department of Education, 2009), but the question is whether Christian formation can take place in online courses (see Lowe & Lowe, 2010). Many theologians argue that spiritual formation and nurture must include bodily presence (Kelsey, 2002). Is it possible that online courses can provide a virtual presence that is commensurate of bodily presence? The Association of Theological Schools (ATS) conducted a study of traditional face to face learning called *Being There*, which expressed concerns regarding new "delivery" systems that are not face to face. Included in the criticism of online education is that theological education in an online context is driven by pragmatics, that schools gravitate to current technologies without due consideration of theological issues. David Kelsey (2002), a proponent for the theological grounding of theological education, raises issues in regard to online education. He questions whether such a theological basis is possible for online education, and whether online education is consistent with a Christian theological anthropology. Kelsey wonders whether online education fosters a spiritualized and dualistic view of human beings as "spiritual machines" that undermines the Christian understanding of human beings as personal bodies whose material bodiness is affirmed by divine creation and incarnation (Gresham, 2006). John Gresham (2006), a Roman Catholic educator, argues for "divine pedagogy as embodiment" and as model for online education. He refutes David Kelsey (2002) and others who claim that online education as theological education is not theologically valid based on dualism and disembodiment. Gresham (2006) argues that the pedagogy of the incarnation points to the realm of the student's life experience as the locus of divine saving action. He argues that *koinonia*, or community, cannot be restricted to physical presence since Paul says we enjoy the fellowship with Christ now (1 Cor. 1:9, New International Version). He insists that when the church celebrates "communion" we experience a *koinonia* with Christ even though he is not physically present (1 Cor. 10:16). Physical, face to face community is not required since the Spirit is active in forming and shaping us into Christlikeness. Also, Mary Hess (2005) challenges the assumption that online education is disembodied, and typical classrooms learning are embodied. She argues that the contextualization of learning in a student's home environment is *incarnational* and *embodied* learning, as compared to artificial and the abstract world of the classroom. Gresham (2006) continues by stating that the divine pedagogy includes a communal dimension similar to the Church, provides active participation of the students in the learning process, and the divine pedagogy is relevant to online education because it is rich in symbols and signs that communicate meaning. The debate about whether Christian formation can take place in online learning communities will continue, but the work of Gresham and others indicate that community can take place in an online context and that the social interaction of presence can provide a context for student's faith to be formed and shaped (Maddix & Estep, 2010).

FACTORS THAT ENHANCE ONLINE LEARNING COMMUNITIES

All online courses are not created equally. There is a wide range of philosophies of and approaches to online courses that may or may not develop online learning communities. Some online courses are designed more like a correspondence course with infrequent student and professor interaction. However, based on the literature and my experience in teaching online courses, courses that are designed with intentional student to student and faculty to student interaction on a regular basis enhance learning and formation. This is reflected in the research by Alfred Rovai (2002), who says that transactional distance, a psychological and communication space between learners and instructors, is reduced when students and faculty engage in more dialogue. He indicates that those who argue against online learning communities do not recognize that the frequency of dialogue enhances learning and community. Also, Mary Shore (2007) argues that this frequency of communication enhances social presence online. Effective online learning communities are fostered by the social presence of both faculty and students. Alfred Rovai (2002) in his study provides the following factors that build and sustain a sense of community:

1. *Transactional Distance.* When dialogue is increased, transactional distance is reduced. Transactional distance is a psychological and communication space between learners and instructors. Rovai argues that in online learning communities this transactional distance is minimized because of the frequency of discussion with students and faculty (Rovai, 2002). Online courses should include requirements for students to be actively engaged in dialogue and discussion on a regular basis.

2. *Social Presence.* The role that social presence plays in online courses is essential in online learning communities to reduce transactional distance. Rovai (2002) argues that communication in online courses must be more intentional than in face-to-face courses since many of the social cues are lost in the online context. When social presence is increased, it enhances community (2001). Also, student satisfaction is higher when the faculty member is active and present in the online course. When the professor is absent from the online dialogue, it creates anxiety for students and inhibits their learning.

3. *Social Equality.* In an online course it is important to get personal information about each student to help ensure equality of gender and voice. This can include the students posting autobiographies about their lives. Rovai refers to this as social equality. Online courses must ensure equal opportunities for participation by all students. He argues that in many traditional classrooms community building is inhibited because of the dominance of men, who are often in the majority (2002). One of the benefits of online courses is that everyone is on the front row and everyone is engaged in the online interaction.

4. *Small group activities* or small groups of learners in online courses enhance collaboration and community. These communities help students make connections with each other (Rovai, 2002). This is especially significant when teaching an online class with more than 20 students. Dividing the class into small groups enhances learning and the development of relationships.

5. *Group Facilitation.* Online courses help faculty members become better facilitators of learning through active listening and humility, which enhances group discussion and promotes community (Rovai, 2001). Professors who teach online are forced to understand adult

learning theory and methods to understand the unique needs of teaching from a distance.

6. *Teaching Style and Stage of Learning.* Online learning communities reflect the wide range of teaching and learning styles of students. Faculty members will need to develop a course that is situational for the needs of the students based on their learning styles. A variety of teaching methodologies and approaches have to be developed to engage the diversity of student needs and learning styles.

7. *Size of Community (course).* The key to developing online learning communities that foster formation is classes that are smaller in size, between 10 and 15 students. Rovai (2002) argues that professors can facilitate small classes for effective learning and formation. According to Rovai (2002), if we can design and deliver online courses that build and sustain community by drawing on these factors, perhaps our actions will help promote satisfaction in e-learning programs.

Those who develop online courses in Christian higher educational institutions will need to assist students in making the necessary adjustments to learning at a distance by enhancing student satisfaction and commitment through the development of a strong sense of community. The development of community has the potential of reversing feelings of isolation through interaction with the professor and other students, which should result in overall student satisfaction and educational success. When these factors are attended to, students will experience a more positive educational experience and will feel part of a dynamic learning community.

BEST PRACTICES IN ONLINE LEARNING COMMUNITIES

From reading the literature and from my personal experience in teaching online classes for the past thirteen years, a variety of best practices emerge in developing online learning communities. When these practices are included in online courses the sense of community and the student to student and professor to student interaction is enhanced. The list of best practices includes the following areas of focus:

1. *Develop clear guidelines for online discussion:* The heart of online learning communities is online discussion and dialogue. It is important to develop a clear discussion board rubric that outlines the criteria for effective discussion. Just because a class requires interaction doesn't mean that it is effective interaction. Effective discussion board rubrics provide an objective way to measure online interaction. The criteria should include critical and thoughtful responses

that are posted on time and should the students' ability to integrate what they are learning in the course. The goal is for students to move beyond lower levels of recall to higher levels of integration and analysis through their responses, as reflected in Benjamin Bloom's taxonomy of learning. Also, the course design should require at least 20% of the course grade to reflect online interaction, and the rubric should be clear about the number of responses required each week between students and the professor. When developing your course requirements for student interaction, try to ensure that there is equal dialogue between student to student, faculty and students, and student to course materials. Here is a list of items to consider when developing guidelines for online discussion:

- Provide a clear online discussion board rubric,
- Post guidelines for communication, including netiquette guidelines,
- Model good communication when posting in the discussion board or via email,
- Explain what constitutes a substantive post in the discussion board,
- Keep daily/weekly records of student responses,
- Send personal critiques to students individually, not in the group,
- Be aware of cultural patterns and preferences,
- Deal with inappropriate responses outside the classroom through personal email,
- Summarize threads to prompt further exploration.,
- Praise students who respond effectively, and
- Be active in the online discussion (social presence is important).

2. *Develop supportive learning environments:* In order for effective online learning communities to develop, students need to feel safe, welcomed, and supported in the online course. Since students are not visible in an online course, often judgments regarding personal appearance are replaced with judging students based on their ability to communicate well through writing. It is important to be sensitive to differences of gender, age, and ethnicity of students who are taking an online course. These cultural differences can often be miscommunicated in an online context. Also, some students will want to dominate the discussion with too many posts or some students will not provide enough student interaction. In either case it is important to communicate to them about what is appropriate in an online class. Similar to a face to face class, how the professor sets the tone and the atmosphere for the online course will determine whether it is a safe place for learning.

3. *Online presence and faculty involvement:* As discussed above it is clear that effective online learning communities are dependent on the involvement of the professor in the online class. The professor is responsible for facilitating the personal and social aspects of an online community in order for the class to have a successful learning experience (Palloff & Pratt, 1999). The best online faculty, according to students, are faculty who show their presence daily in a course. Professors who do not have a regular presence in a course negatively impact student learning and satisfaction in the course. Most online courses require that the professor respond to the student within a 24 hour time frame. Another important aspect of faculty involvement is providing ample feedback to class discussion and course assignments. Since many online courses are accelerated, it is critical that professors give timely feedback.

   Also, it is essential for the professor to be intentional about making relational connections with students. The student and professor should post autobiographies that provide information about each student's life, faith journey, hobbies, and interests. A picture of the student can also be included on his or her personal home page. Professors can make personal calls to students and/or connect with them through Skype or Adobe.Connect or other social mediums as a way to get better acquainted with students. These relationship opportunities foster community among students and the professor, which enhances learning and formation.

4. *Create learning activities that foster interaction and dialogue:* Consistent with the face to face classroom, online students will get out of a learning community what they put into it. If they are passive and choose not to engage in community, then the benefits they derive will be limited (Vesely et al., 2007). Professors play a key role in motivating students to be engaged in online discussion and dialogue by recognizing the diverse learning styles of students and by providing a variety of learning activities in the course. These learning activities, which are similar in scope to face to face courses, include developing collaborative and team learning, small groups, and contextualized assignments to ensure that students are engaged in dynamic forms of interaction.

The implementation of these practices will ensure that effective online learning communities will foster student and professor interaction in online courses. It will also ensure that both the professor and student will have a meaningful learning experience that fosters effective learning and formation.

CONCLUSION

As institutions in Christian higher education continue to develop online courses, they will want to ensure that effective learning and Christian formation is taking place in online courses. The professor's modeling of effective communication through active participation, along with a clear discussion board rubric will ensure students' development of learning and social interaction. When professors and students engage in dynamic learning communities that foster consistent dialogue and discussion, students will feel more connected and supported in their learning. When this takes place, the concern about embodied learning is reduced and allows for students and faculty to engage in collaborative learning experiences. These learning experiences provide a context for students to be formed and shaped through the influence of their Christian professors and classmates.

DISCUSSION QUESTIONS

1. How do you foster online learning communities in online courses? What are essential characteristics necessary to ensure effective student and faculty interaction?
2. Why are online learning communities important for institutions of Christian higher education? How can they ensure that Christian formation is taking place in online courses?
3. Why is it important for you and your institution to develop online learning communities?
4. What are the essential criteria in developing an online discussion board rubric? How can you determine if effective interaction is taking place in an online course?
5. Since the presence of the professor is critical in effective learning and in developing online learning communities, what role does the professor play in ensuring that community is established? What are some essential characteristics necessary to ensure faculty presence in an online course?
6. Based on the list of best practices for developing online learning communities, what are areas of strength and areas that need improvement?

REFERENCES

Allen, I. E. & Seaman, J. (2010). *Learning on demand: Online education in the United States.* Retrieved from http://www.sloanconsortium.org/publications/survey/pdf/learningondemand.pdf

Cannell, L. (1999). A review of literature on distance education. *Theological Education, 36*(1), 172.

Carr, S. (2000). As distance education comes to age, the challenge is keeping the students. *The Chronicle of Higher Education, 46*(23), A39–A41.

Gresham, J. (2006). Divine pedagogy as a model for online education. *Teaching Theology and Religion, 9*(1), 24–28.

Hess, M. (2005). *Engaging technology in theological education. All that we cannot leave behind.* Lanham, MD: Rowman and Littlefield Publishers, Inc.

Kelsey, D. H. (2002). Spiritual machines, personal bodies and God: Theological education and theological anthropology. *Teaching Theology and Religion, 5*(1), 2–9.

Lowe, M. & Lowe, S. (2010). Spiritual formation in theological distance education: An ecosystems model. *Christian Education Journal, 7*(3), 85–102.

Maddix, M. & Estep, J. (2010). Spiritual formation in online higher education communities: Nurturing spirituality in Christian higher education online degree programs. *Christian Education Journal, 7*(2), 423–436.

Palloff, R. M. & Pratt, K. (1999). *Building learning communities in cyberspace: Effective strategies for the online classroom.* San Francisco: Jossey-Bass.

Palloff, R. M. & Pratt, K. (2007). *Building online learning communities: Effective strategies for the virtual classroom.* San Francisco: Jossey-Bass.

Rovai, A. P. (2002). Building a sense of community at a distance. *International Review of Research in Open and Distant Learning, 3*(1), 1–16.

Shea, P., Sau Li, C., & Pickett, A. (2006). A study of teaching presence and student sense of learning community in fully online and web-enhanced college courses. *Internet and Higher Education, 9*(3), 175–190.

Shore, M. H. (2007). Establishing social presence in online courses: Why and How. *Theological Education, 42*(2), 91–100.

United States Department of Education. (2009). *Evaluation of Evidence-Based Practices in Online Learning: A Meta-Analysis and Review of Online Learning Studies.* Retrieved from http://www2.ed.gov/rschstat/eval/tech/evidence-based-practices/finalreport.pdf

Vesely, P., Bloom, L., & Sherlock, J. (2007). Key elements in building online communities: Comparing faculty and student perceptions. *MERLOT Journal of Online Teaching and Learning, 3*(3).

CHAPTER 4

SOCIAL PRESENCE IN ONLINE LEARNING

Stephen Kemp
BILD International

Fifteen years ago, many academic leaders thought it was impossible for students to have truly meaningful community interaction in an online distance education environment. Ironically, one of the biggest struggles today for many traditional campus professors is to keep their students off Facebook during class! This chapter focuses on the research and practice on how *distance* can be broken down in online learning and how *presence* can be supported and optimized in online and real life social contexts. Specifically, this chapter places the consideration of social presence in online learning in its historical context, addresses learning theory and research, and provides practical recommendations.

HISTORICAL CONTEXT OF SOCIAL PRESENCE IN ONLINE LEARNING

Online learning emerged from a century-long procession of distance education technologies. For most of its history, the practice of distance educa-

Best Practices of Online Education, pages 41–53
Copyright © 2012 by Information Age Publishing

41

tion has focused on accessible content delivery. Correspondence programs delivered course content to students in the form of workbooks. Radio and audiotapes delivered faculty lectures. Television and videotapes delivered a visual replication of the classroom and classroom resources. Floppy disks delivered similar content in a very compact manner for use on a computer, sometimes including feedback, such as self-grading quizzes and email interaction with faculty. Some of the first online programs replicated the computer disc-based courses through the use of websites. Another form of online learning, the mentored online seminar course, emerged as the most common genre in use today.

Distance education has operated mostly in the shadows of traditional higher education until recently. It is only mentioned incidentally, if at all, in standard higher education histories by Jencks and Reisman, Rudolph, Veysey, and Thelin. Distance education seems to have been tolerated as serving a good function, particularly for those who could not come to a campus and for those on vocational non-degree certification tracks. Until the emergence of online learning programs, there were only a few large distance education programs, but many small programs serving niche markets. According to The Sloan Consortium, in Fall 2009, 5.5 million students, 29.3% of total enrollment in the United States, were taking at least one online course (Allen & Seaman, 2010). The largest higher education institutions in the world are now characterized by online learning. Two Christian institutions are listed in the Top 10 Colleges with Largest Online Enrollments, 2010 at www.top10onlineuniversities.org. The University of Phoenix has 400,000 online students, Liberty University has 55,000, and Grand Canyon University has 35,000 (Chronicle of Higher Education, 2010). According to *Baker's Guide to Christian Online Learning* (2011), more than 125 Christian colleges, universities, and seminaries offer degrees online.

Academic discussion at the end of the twentieth century about the legitimacy of distance education was largely represented by 355 studies showing that there was no significant difference between traditional campus-based education and distance education (Russell, 1999). This was recognized as good news for distance education, but it was short-lived because of the increased emphasis on the central role of interactivity in higher education. Russell's collection of research focused almost entirely on comparisons of content delivery. The new questions about legitimacy were related to formation and interactivity in a learning community.

Social presence, defined as a learning community characterized by interactivity between students and faculty, emerged as a primary concern of most accrediting agencies, including the Association of Theological Schools (ATS), and distance education regulations became more restrictive. "Because of the formational requirements of most ATS degree programs, and the perceived relationship between intentional community and formation, not more than one-third of the total credits required for completion of an ATS-approved degree can be earned by external independent study" (Association of Theological Schools, 1996, n.p.). The assumption by accreditors that it was impossible to have true learning community through technologically-mediated forms led many distance educators to fear the impending demise of their programs. However, minimum standards for interactivity in distance education courses emerged, and creative attempts to comply were developed. For instance, one provider of independent courses to ATS-recognized seminaries provided a general forum in which students of various seminaries could interact with each other in an online discussion forum. Another ATS-recognized institution developed online discussion forums for each of its disciplinary departments.

Advances in distance education technology often came with the promise of bringing dramatic change to education, most notably by Thomas Edison. "Books will soon be obsolete in the schools. Scholars will soon be instructed through the eye. It is possible to teach every branch of human knowledge with the motion picture. Our school system will be completely changed within ten years" (Smith, 1913, p. 24). However, these dramatic changes have not been seen. "What often passes as innovative uses of instructional technologies is generally grounded in a marriage uniting eighteenth-century models of learning with nineteenth-century notions of organizational management" (Privateer, 1999, p. 60). This is clearly seen in the emergence in the late 1990s of for-profit companies, such as Real Education, who advertised that they could "create your online campus in 60 days—guaranteed," but focused almost entirely on creating online forms of traditional campus functions. Christian institutions tried to create online versions of classrooms, student lounges, prayer rooms, and chapels. Yet, in light of Edison's bold claims and Russell's touting of research, Saba asks the poignant question, "Now that we have spent millions of dollars setting up production systems, computer servers, and telecommunications infrastructure, what can we do with them that was not possible to do with a chalk and a blackboard?" (Saba, cited in Russell, 1999, p. 2).

The mentored online seminar has emerged as a new genre of distance education course that goes beyond what is possible in a traditional classroom, particularly in terms of social presence. For instance, online students may participate in discussion through asynchronous threaded forums (described more fully in the Best Practices section of this chapter). This means that students may post comments in a structured manner that allows them to be more thoughtful and deliberative, not just quick and impulsive. It allows (and usually requires) that all students participate substantively in each discussion because there is no place to hide or be overlooked. Conversations can last throughout the entire course, not just during a brief window of time. It is even possible to search for key words that have been written or retrieve any statement or conversation that anyone has written during the entire course. Vibrant and substantive personal interaction between students and faculty is a hallmark of the mentored online seminar course.

Interestingly, the earliest description of this genre that I have been able to find in any higher education publication was in a 1995 issue of *Technological Horizons in Education*. It was written by Raymond Albrektson (1995) about an online church history course of Toccoa Falls Bible College. "It is apparent that the model of mentored-seminar, an educational model that dates back to Socrates and Plato, has enormous flexibility and educational integrity in its online form.... This model makes great use of our greatest educational resources—motivated students—and has great potential for fulfilling the promise of online education in a cost-effective, human-centered form" (Albrektson, 1995, p. 105). Even traditional campus courses are utilizing the tools of online learning. Research today on online learning, such as the recent evaluation of online learning research by the U.S. Department of Education, includes a focus on "blended learning," which essentially is the use of online learning tools in traditional campus courses and/or the use of some traditional classroom lecture in online courses (Means, Toyama, Murphy, Bakia, & Jones, 2010). Perhaps Edison's promise for dramatic change in education is actually coming to fruition.

Whether one can have truly meaningful community interaction in an online environment is largely a question of the past. We now live in a world that is being shaped by the use of nearly ubiquitous online communication (e.g., uprisings in North Africa). However, the question remains whether the social presence of online learning as manifested in the similarly ubiquitous mentored online seminar is sufficient to accomplish the objectives of Christian higher education courses and programs. This will be addressed in the next section on Learning Theory.

LEARNING THEORY AND SOCIAL PRESENCE

Concern for social presence has often been at the center of distance education learning theory, most notably through Michael Moore's (1997) work on transactional distance. His theory of distance education focuses on the variables of Dialogue, Structure, and Learner Autonomy to describe the interactions that take place for a student in a distance education environment (Moore, 1997). Moore quotes Saba's systems dynamics hypothesis to summarize: "When structure increases, transactional distance increases and dialog decreases. When dialog increases, transactional distance decreases and structure decreases." However, as Saba also notes, "with new interactive technology we have potential for dialog between learners and a new form of learner-learner autonomy reducing the transactional distance for each student" (Saba, cited in Moore, 2006, n.p.). Thus, because mentored online seminar courses increase both structure and dialogue, transactional distance is significantly decreased and social presence is significantly increased.

The potential for online learning was at the foundation of Palloff and Pratt's (1999) early work, *Building Learning Communities in Cyberspace*, which was a guide for making the transition from the traditional classroom to the online environment. At the core of their work is "a defining and redefining" of the concept of community in education (Palloff & Pratt, 1999, p. 25). Because they hold that "the learning community is the vehicle through which learning occurs online" (pp. 29–30), even their diagrammed framework of distance learning has "community" at the center. In a follow-up book, they focus on collaboration as the expression of community. They recognize that community needs to exist in order for collaboration to occur, but "that collaboration activity can also help to develop that sense of community, thus enabling the creation of an environment in which further collaborative work can happen" (Palloff & Pratt, 2005, pp. 4–5). Half of their book is given to a wide variety of collaborative activities for online learning, such as role playing, blogs, and webquests in which most of the information comes from the web.

Key social roles are redefined in online learning. In many cases, the faculty member as a facilitator of learning is emphasized more than as an expert dispenser of content. This is particularly true for the mentored online seminar course. In Salmon's (2000) model of online teaching and learning, the key is the faculty member as e-moderator. Learning increases with the amount and type of interactivity facilitated by the e-moderator (Salmon, 2000). Conrad and Donaldson (2011) focus on the learning activities of the online classroom. During a typical course, the instructor's role moves from social negotiator to structural engineer to facilitator to community member/challenger. The learner's role moves from newcomer to cooperator to collaborator to initiator/partner as learners initiate activities for the class (Conrad & Donaldson, 2011). Similarly, Ko and Rossen (2010) emphasis classroom management, particularly in terms of facilitation of the learning experience for students. Shelton and Saltsman extend the concept of engagement to participation in online student government (2005). Nearly one-third of the ideas in Hanna's *147 Practical Tips for Teaching Online Groups* deal with matters of social presence and interaction (Hanna, Conceição-Runlee, & Glowacki-Dudka, 2000).

Perhaps the most significant aspect of learning theory related to social presence in online learning is related to the very definition of distance education firmly established by Moore and others. Traditionally, distance education has focused on technological mediation of the separation of teacher and learner. This concept is turned upside down by Marianne Mount (2008) in her dissertation titled "Presence in Distance: The Lived Experience of

Faith Formation in an Online Learning Community." Mount refreshingly defines distance education in terms of what is present for the learner rather than what is absent. She asks "what is the lived experience of adult faith formation in an online learning community?" and seeks "to uncover presence in the life-world of distance education, as dwelling within technology, as richness in absence, as solitude, silence, text, home, place, time, and community" (2008, p. 82). Gibson (1998) devotes an entire chapter of her early book called *Distance Learners in Higher Education* to "The Distance Learner in Context." She states that "as we look at the distance learner, we must remember that these learners exist in a broad social context—a social context which can profoundly affect the success of the distance teaching-learning transaction" (Gibson, 1998, p. 113). Ormond Simpson's (2003) research on retention of students of the Open University demonstrates that family and friends are the most important source of external support, greater than tutors, other students, employers, and the institution. He claims that "it appears that the most important single form of support for Open University students is outside institutional control (and may be largely ignored by institutions)" (Simpson, 1999, p. 121). In my recent article in *Christian Education Journal*, I attempt to explain the educational theory of situated learning and practical examples of how real life learning communities can be used to optimize academic objectives (Kemp, 2010).

For Christian educators, social presence is not just a means to an academic end, but a foundational component of Christian education itself. In expressing reservation about advances in distance education of seminaries, ATS researchers wrote, "If those devising new forms were to find ways to duplicate or improve on the processes that we have mapped that are a function of being on site, our concerns would dissipate" (Carroll, Wheeler, Aleshire, & Marler, 1997, pp. 276–277). Particularly noteworthy among the responses are Steve and Mary Lowe, who have provided an ecosystem model to help us consider the full range of dimensions of community and spiritual formation for online learners, including social networks outside of the traditional academic learning community (Lowe & Lowe, 2010a). Further, they have provided an instrument that measures and stimulates fulfillment of the biblical "one another" commands, both in the online learning environment and in real life social contexts (Lowe & Lowe, 2010b). Jeff Reed of BILD International has also provided extremely valuable tools, such as the "Becoming Established" assessment form that allows one's spiritual foundation to be examined according to apostolic statements of what it means to be established in your faith, as well as a continuum on which to recognize the unique contributions of truly church-based theological education (Reed, 2001).

In my 2008 presidential address to ACCESS, the Christian distance education association, I congratulated our organization on the fact that we have arrived because of the educational quality of our distance education programs. However, I also cautioned us about being content because there may be other destinations at which we should arrive. If we are going to take social presence seriously, then perhaps we should not be content with the vibrant online community of mentored online seminars alone. Perhaps we should strive for even more, as described by Lowe, Mount, myself, and others. A few suggestions will be given in the next section under the subheading of Next Practices.

BEST PRACTICES

In this section, I will address best practices related to social presence in online learning based on my experience. I will start with a description of several common practices that are widely accepted, but may not necessarily represent best practices. I will also identify several worst practices that should probably be avoided. Then, I will address what I consider to be truly best practices as currently manifested in better online learning programs. Lastly, I will provide a few suggestions of what I consider to be next best practices, by which I mean best practices that may not yet be in use even by the better online learning programs.

Common Practices

In mentored online seminars, it is common to use threaded discussion forums in which the professor (or designer of the course) posts discussion starters for each lesson. These often are related to the reading assignments or video lecture for the lesson. In my research of online learning, many courses simply instruct students to post their initial responses and respond substantively (whatever that means) two to three times to the postings of others.

In larger online courses, it is common to break the groups into smaller units for the purpose of having manageable discussion, depending on the quantity of forums and frequency of expectations for posting. Generally, if there are more than 15 students, it is common to structure their interaction in smaller groups rather than as a whole class.

In online independent study courses, it is common to give students assignments to do critical thinking and creative application regarding the lesson content, not just assignments focused directly on content acquisition. Students seem much more likely to retain the content if they are also doing these other things.

Most online learning programs provide basic guidance with regard to *netiquette* (proper behavior in online environments). This includes things like not using capital letters for whole words unless you are intending to shout and being careful in making curt responses and using sarcasm because they can easily misunderstood in online environments.

Most online learning programs encourage faculty and students to post personal information and links to personal websites, Facebook, Twitter, and the like. It is important to establish personal connections early in the course so that students can establish points of contact and context for their interactions. Active participation by the faculty facilitator usually sets the tone for the social presence of the course.

Additionally, the social presence of a course is enhanced greatly by having accessible support services. The tone of a class discussion is often closely related to the other aspects of service provided by the online learning institution, such as ease of access to online reading materials.

Worst Practices

A few online learning platforms have very rudimentary discussions forums that are really not much more than linear blogs. While these are inexpensive platforms to administer, they are also difficult to use for real discussion because there is no ability to track multiple discussions within a lesson. Blogs are also difficult to use if they do not have a mechanism to mark what has been read. As the course proceeds, it can be very cumbersome to scroll through long lists in order to find the new posts. Blog-type discussions do not usually foster much interaction or create much social presence for the class.

Some online learning programs have tried to replicate traditional campus facilities online, such as student lounges, chapels, and prayer rooms. In large measure, these have not been effective. In fact, they are infrequently used unless required in some manner by the institution. The concern for these things is noble, but it tends to fail to recognize that distance education students are older, more independent, and established in real life social contexts (families, neighborhoods, churches) that actually provide better forms of these services. Student lounges, chapels, and prayer rooms were created on campuses largely because so many students are living on campus apart from their families, neighborhoods, and churches.

Best Practices

In mentored online seminars, students complete reading assignments and/or view video lectures, post initial responses in a threaded discussion forum to a question from a faculty member, post additional responses in discussion with students and the faculty member, and complete other course-length assignments, such as papers and tests also administered on-line. It is best to give additional guidance regarding the threaded discussion forum. For instance, if lessons are to be completed weekly, students should be expected to make their initial postings early in the week so that there is plenty of time for "substantive" response later in the week.

Another best practice is to give specific expectations for the length of responses. This prevents students from simply posting "I agree" or "nice post." It also helps to control the prolific posters who write mini-dissertations for each response.

In larger classes that use small groups for much of the interaction on lessons, it is often good to have some forums for the entire class to participate together. This is particularly helpful for the facilitator to give content or guidance to the entire class without having to post in each small group. It also can be used to help students find affinity with other students.

Advanced *netiquette* helps students to know how to avoid unnecessary conflict by not using inflammatory language, personal attacks, jumping to conclusions, antagonistic responses, and so on. It also teaches students how to use constructive approaches to disagreement, such as asking questions for the sake of learning rather than arguing or making your own point more clear. Further, it is good to give guidance on how to resolve conflict or misunderstanding once it happens, such as posting apologies, moving the discussion from the public forum to private email or phone, and relying on the faculty facilitator to monitor the interaction.

Faculty facilitators need to take the lead in presenting personal information about themselves and making personal connections with students. If they do so early in the course, it sets the pace for the social presence of the course for everyone. The more engaged the faculty member is, the more robust the social presence of the course is likely to be.

A best practice in online learning is to be committed as an institution to being online 24/7. This means that faculty facilitators need to be present often. If they are posting daily, students are much more likely to be checking daily. Faculty facilitators also need to provide means for students to have prompt, personal interaction with other students as needed by phone or personal email addresses. Further, the institution itself needs to do everything it can to avoid being offline. Seamless administrative and technological service is often underestimated in terms of its importance to the overall social presence of the course.

Online learning institutions can also provide support for faculty facilitators. Part-time staff can monitor the discussion forums and alert the faculty facilitator to jump in at particular places. They can also track inactive students to identify problems and encourage their participation in the course (and retention for the program).

A best practice of online learning institutions is to establish cohorts, not just offer courses. One of the limitations of non-cohort programs is that even though vibrant learning communities are established in individual courses, they usually have to be rebuilt with each new course. Cohorts allow learning communities to be carried from one course to another and built throughout the program.

Next Practices

In mentored online seminars, it is even better to give specific direction to help responses in the threaded discussion board to be substantive. For instance, students can be assigned to respond to the initial posting of another student whose post fits particular criteria, such as most similar, most different, most helpful, most intriguing, most challenging, and so on. Or responses can be made on the basis of personal relation, such as to someone who is at a similar (or different) age, occupation, place of life, or other characteristic. Other direction can call for students to respond to the posts with which they most agree (adding rationale that the student may not have included) or disagree (focusing on the rationale, not making personal attacks or dismissive comments). Students can also be instructed to respond in a particular manner, such as with humor, sarcasm, encouragement. A variety of responses can be built into the course in order to add to the variety and effectiveness of the interaction, but also to help students develop in a wide range of communication techniques.

Often, threaded email discussions in classes with more than 10 students can become rather difficult for students to manage because of the magnitude of postings. Rather than simply break the class into small groups, it may be more effective to help students create a buddy system. Essentially, they should read and interact with everything that is posted in response to their initial post in each thread. They should also pick a few other students as "buddies" for whom they will read and interact with everything that is posted in threads started by them. And, of course, they should read and respond as necessary to anything posted by the faculty member who is facilitating the course.

Tools such as Lowe's "one another" assessment or BILD International's "becoming established" assessment can be used powerfully to enhance social presence according to biblical standards. Simply putting these tools in places where they can be used as standards by which we look at social presence is powerful.

In online independent study courses, it is good to include collaborative activities. This can be done with students who are enrolled at the same time. Or it can be done by pushing students to engage in learning activities with those around them, even if they are not enrolled. This is particularly valuable for learning that is likely to take place better in a real life context than in an abstract academic environment.

Further, online independent study courses can be designed with components that wrap-around the social context of the students. For instance, an enrolled married student can be expected to have interaction on the course material with their unenrolled spouse and reflect on that interaction in written assignments. Rather than letting the course be something that drives a couple apart so that one can study, these assignments draw the couple together. Of course, they need to be done with sensitivity and flexibility to the busyness and interests of the unenrolled spouse. Similarly, students can be expected to have interactions with pastors, ministry leaders, and even unbelievers regarding the content of their courses. One of the potential tragedies of many online learning programs is that students can take courses in spiritual formation (or even graduate from entire degree programs) without their pastors even knowing that they are enrolled.

Similarly, in mentored online seminar courses, students should not just be asked to post and respond to each other. Perhaps they should be required to have particular interactions with those in their real life learning communities (pastors, ministry leaders, family members, neighbors, friends, unbelieving co-workers, etc.) based on the material of the lesson, and then post their thoughts that include reflection on these interactions. This turns the threaded discussion forum into a venue for processing growth in real life situations and primary social relationships rather than just having an abstract academic conversation.

In conclusion, it is clear that social presence is a crucial dimension of effective online learning. This chapter has focused on how *distance* can be broken down in online learning and how *presence* can be supported and optimized in online and real life social contexts. Hopefully the consideration of historical perspective, learning theory, and best practices (especially next best practices) can be used to stimulate improvement for weak programs and to strengthen programs that are already strong.

DISCUSSION QUESTIONS

1. To what degree are you still fighting the philosophical battles over the legitimacy of online education? Were you aware of how widespread and successful it has become?
2. How well are you drawing on the resources related to research on history, learning theory, and best practices? What did you identify that you could use to improve your program?

3. What forms of online learning are you using? Are you taking advantage of mentored online seminar format? How are you intentionally designing your programs to take advantage of the potential of social presence in online learning?
4. How do your distance education practices compare to the common, worst, best, and next practices described in this chapter? What would you add or delete from these lists? What areas have you identified in your program for improvement?

REFERENCES

Albrektson, J. R. (1995). Mentored online seminar: A model for graduate-level distance learning. *Technological Horizons in Education Journal, 23*(3), 102–105.

Allen, I. E. & Seaman, J. (2010). *Class Differences: Online Education in the United States, 2010.* Newburyport, MA: Babson Survey Research Group and The Sloan Consortium.

Association of Theological Schools. (1996). Final report on the redeveloped accrediting standards. *Theological Education, 32*(2), 1–143.

Baker, J. (2011). *Baker's Guide to Christian Online Learning.* Retrieved on July 6, 2011, from www.bakersguide.com/directory

Carroll, J. W., Wheeler, B. G., Aleshire, D. O., & Marler, P. L. (1997). *Being there: Culture and formation in two theological schools.* Oxford: Oxford University Press.

The Chronicle of Higher Education, Online Learning. (2010, November). Virtual Education Goes Mainstream. Washington, DC: Author.

Conrad, R., & Donaldson, J. A. (2011). *Engaging the Online Learner: Activities and Resources for Creative Instruction.* San Francisco: John Wiley and Sons.

Gibson, C. C. (1998). *Distance learners in higher education: Institutional responses for quality outcomes.* Madison, WI: Atwood.

Hanna, D. E., Conceição-Runlee, S., & Glowacki-Dudka, M. (2000). *147 Practical Tips for Teaching Online Groups: Essentials of Web-Based Education.* Madison, WI: Atwood.

Kemp, S. J. (2010). Situated learning: Optimizing experiential learning through God-given learning community. *Christian Education Journal (Series 3), 7*(2), 118–143.

Ko, S., & Rossen, S. (2010). *Teaching online: A practical guide.* New York: Routledge.

Lowe, S. D., & Lowe, M. E. (2010a). Spiritual formation in theological distance education: An ecosystems model. *Christian Education Journal (Series 3), 7*(1), 85–102.

Lowe, S. D., & Lowe, M. E. (2010b). *Allelon:* Reciprocal commands and Christian development. *Christian Education Journal (Series 3), 7*(2), 281–298.

Means, B., Toyama, Y., Murphy, R., Bakia, M., & Jones, K. (2010). *Evaluation of Evidence-Based Practices in Online Learning: A Meta-Analysis and Review of Online Learning Studies.* U.S. Department of Education, Office of Planning, Evaluation, and Policy Development, Policy and Program Studies Service. Retrieved on July 6, 2011, from www2.ed.gov/rschstat/eval/tech/evidence-based-practices/finalreport.pdf.

Moore, M. G. (1997). Theory of Transactional Distance. In D. Keegan (Ed.), *Theoretical Principles of Distance Education* (pp. 22–38). New York: Routledge.

Moore, M. G. (2006). Evolution of Theory of Transactional Distance. Presentation to the European Distance Education Network. (October 27). Retrieved on July 6, 2011, from www.eden-online.org/contents/conferences/research/ . . . / Michael_Moore.ppt.

Mount, M. (2008). *Presence in distance: The lived experience of adult faith formation in an online learning community* (Unpublished doctoral dissertation). Virginia Polytechnic University, Blacksburg, VA.

Palloff, R. M., & Pratt, K. (1999). *Building learning communities in cyberspace: Effective strategies for the online classroom.* San Francisco, CA: Jossey-Bass.

Privateer, P. M. (1999). Academic technology and the future of higher education: Strategic paths taken and not taken. *Journal of Higher Education, 70*(1), 60–79.

Reed, J. (2001, January). *Church-based ministry training that is truly church-based.* Paper presented at the ACCESS annual conference, Chicago, IL.

Russell, T. L. (1999). *The no significant difference phenomenon: A comparative research annotated bibliography on technology for distance education as reported in 355 research reports, summaries and papers.* Montgomery, AL: The International Distance Education Certification Center.

Salmon, G. (2000). *E-moderating: The key to teaching and learning online.* London: Kogan Page.

Shelton, K., & Saltsman G. (2005). *An administrator's guide to online education.* Greenwich, CT: Information Age Publishing.

Simpson, O. (1999). *Supporting students in online, open and distance learning.* London: Kogan Page.

Simpson, O. (2003). *Student retention in online, open and distance learning.* London: Kogan Page.

Smith, F. J. (1913, July 9). The Evolution of the Motion Picture, Part VI—Looking Into the Future with Thomas A. Edison. *The New York Dramatic Mirror*, pp. 24 and 42. Retrieved July 6, 2011, from http://fultonhistory.com/Newspaper%2010/New%20York%20NY%20Dramatic%20Mirror/New%20York%20NY%20Dramatic%20Mirror%201913%20Mar-Apr%201914%20Grayscale/New%20York%20NY%20Dramatic%20Mirror%201913%20Mar-Apr%20 1914%20Grayscale%20-%200690.pdf

CHAPTER 5

SPIRITUAL FORMATION AS WHOLE-PERSON DEVELOPMENT IN ONLINE EDUCATION

Mary E. Lowe
Erskine Theological Seminary

Some people find their research for dissertation projects dull or tedious. My experience was just the opposite. The topic of my study focused on the impact of online courses on spiritual formation of students in theological distance education. One of the findings in this study was that spiritual formation was identified in relation to other dimensions such as social and intellectual development. For example, several students commented that a deeper understanding of God contributed to growth spiritually. Additionally, the communal nature of the online course was an important component of spiritual formation. One person noted, "It [my spiritual formation] was impacted greatly through the dialogue with others." What these findings and others suggest is that opportunities for growth and formation are not limited to face-to-face gatherings. The information following further elaborates on these points, and I invite you to join me in exploring this topic together.

Best Practices of Online Education, pages 55–63

SPIRITUAL FORMATION

One of the critical aspects of examining the issue of spiritual formation in online education is the issue of definition. Accreditation bodies are driving institutions toward an outcomes-based assessment, and part of the problem for both parties has been an inability to adequately define spiritual formation. Some of that problem lies in denominational differences, while other obstacles lie in what we mean by spiritual formation. The language that has been used includes terms such as *spirituality, spiritual formation, spiritual growth and development,* and *faith,* somewhat interchangeably. Compounding the problem is that various faith traditions are tied to their own notions of what it means to mature spiritually. The problem is that we persist in using language that describes or refers only to the spiritual dimension. If we are going to move forward in adequately defining spiritual formation, we need to come at the topic from a different perspective that gets away from the limitations identified above. One of the ways in which this can be done is to come at the subject from a whole person perspective that includes an ecosystem model of growth and development. An ecological view looks at the whole person in an interrelated fashion rather than a compartmentalized notion that has historically dominated the discussion. The following expands this idea.

A view toward spiritual formation as whole-person formation is part of what Ward (1995) describes as an integrated person. He compared the process of spiritual formation to an ecological system of human development. He asserted that the five domains—(a) physical, (b) intellectual, (c) emotional, (d) social, and (e) moral—serve as empirical inputs and outputs that help people assess spiritual formation. Each of these components works in an interrelated system of development. If we assume this model to be true, we can make assumptions about spiritual formation based on what we observe in the other dimensions. In fact, spiritual development researchers like Fowler (1981) assert that in order to have a proper understanding of spiritual formation, one cannot separate the spiritual dimension out from the others. The spiritual dimension serves to integrate the other aspects of human life rather than remaining independent of them. Roehlkepartain (Roehlkepartain, King, Wagener, & Benson, 2006) attested to this by stating, "spirituality by its very nature begs us to take a holistic view of persons" (p. 181). If we look at the example of Jesus, we see this same principle to be true. He matured as a whole person in that he grew intellectually, physically, spiritually, and socially (Luke 2:52, New International Version). This is no less true for us.

An Ecological Perspective of Spiritual Formation

One framework for understanding spiritual formation is based on an ecological perspective. The ecosystem we see in nature reflects an interdependence and interaction that sustains viability. Plants, insects, and other entities regulate the flow of inputs and outputs through reciprocal forms of interaction and accommodation. Viewing nature from this perspective allows us to see the connections between individual elements and the whole entity. This is underscored in Worster's (1998) work describing ecology as a relational discipline, using examples to describe the inescapable reality of connectedness. He notes other authors who observe the fact that there is no individualism in ecosystems like nature. Survivability depends on symbiosis. In like fashion, human development follows similar patterns of behavior. The majority of us are not stranded on a deserted island but rather, are part of an interconnected system of social networks. What we learn intellectually in the academy usually influences us spiritually, socially, and morally. We live and operate in community and as a result, we manifest implications of that by our development and growth.

An ecosystem view of spiritual development has advantages for the Christian educator and student. We see this ecological framework in the paradigm of the Body of Christ. We live in a fragmented, fallen world, but the connections we have within the Body of Christ provide a coherence that guards against environmental destruction. Worster (1998) uses the example of a tree that experiences adversities brought about by any number of influences. What sustains the tree is its location in a forest of other trees because while individually, the tree may lose some of its own characteristics, it survives in part because other trees provide what it needs to thrive. As members of the Body of Christ, we thrive because of the *one-anotherness* we experience collectively.

Not only does the Apostle Paul help us understand this ecology, but the parables that Jesus used reflect an ecological perspective of growth. Just as nature reflects natural ecology, human development unfolds in an ecological manner. Spiritual development follows the same patterns that we see in nature. When Jesus referenced something about the Kingdom of God, He used examples in nature as a way of explaining growth and development (Mark 4:26–32; Matt. 6:28).

Fostering Human Development

One way to better understand this approach to defining spiritual formation from an ecological perspective is to look at work in human growth and development theories. Bronfenbrenner (1979) is one such researcher who presents theories in understanding how people mature, making use of a systems approach. Researchers like him are replacing dichotomies between nature and nurture with a more integrative orientation that looks at reciprocal relationships between living organism and ecosystem. Although individual innate patterns of development play a role, they do so in relationship to and in interaction with various settings such as family, school, church, and voluntary organizations. Normal development, according to these social scientists, cannot be done apart from interaction with others.

Many of the complaints about Christian distance education have to do with the absence of face-to-face encounters thought necessary for spiritual formation to occur. What human ecology theories tell us is that whole person development (intellectual, social, moral, emotional, psychological, and spiritual) is *instigated* through social interactions of limitless varieties that take place across the continuum of our ecosystems. Spiritual development as the process of sanctification unfolds across a variety of settings including those interactions that are part of an online course. Persons who are studying online have a common bond of connection that transcends physical time and space.

The interaction of one's social network is at the heart of *Connected: The Surprising Power of Our Social Networks and How They Shape Our Lives.* In this book, Cristakis and Fowler (2009) outline the ways in which even the most distant connection we may have with another person can influence behavior, thoughts, and even spiritual development. Essentially, our social connections, be they immediate or distant, have a powerful influence both in the way we act and in the way we influence others. Furthermore, this social connection is a natural output of something more fundamental, which they see to be related to a spiritual inclination. They argue that "religious sensibilities are partially hardwired in our brains, and they are related to our desire for social connection to others, not only a spiritual connection to God" (Cristakis & Fowler, 2009, p. 246). The real tragedy of Babel, according to Christakis and Fowler, was the disconnection brought about by a willful act of replacing God with self. The citizens were united in their effort to build a tower that would reach to the heavens, but their punishment, confusion of language, resulted in being scattered or disconnected at a fundamental level, which was the ability to communicate. Without the ability to communicate, the community was fragmented.

Online social learning ecologies are powerful contributors to our growth and development. Those that manifest a diversity of experiences, interactions, modes of course delivery, student populations, learning styles, spiritual disciplines, and viewpoints can only facilitate whole person development that mirrors the fullness of Christ. An ecological perspective on spiritual formation in Christian distance education permits us to consider the totality of contexts and settings in which students study, learn, and grow. Rather than delimiting spiritual formation to a face-to-face community, an ecological perspective broadens our appreciation for the multiple social environments in which the Spirit operates to accomplish transformation into the fullness of Christ. Learners who study online are part of other communities in which they interact and in so doing, impact those online groups who in turn reciprocate opportunities for growth and formation. Some may view distance or online education as a process in which isolation and alienation from others occurs. This is, in many respects, a simplistic view of an ecological model of human development. An ecological view of development understands that all these connections, as well as the continual growth of human dimensions, provides clearer understanding of formational opportunities in online learning.

THE ECOLOGY OF ONLINE LEARNING COMMUNITIES

From this perspective, we recognize that student experiences in theological distance education are among many contexts and settings where students have their faith influenced while the student influences the settings and contexts in which they are involved. In an analysis conducted by Palka (2004) of Concordia Seminary, students were asked to define their community in relation to influence on formation. The aspect of their self-described community receiving the highest percentage of responses was "church/pastor" at almost 24%. Other responses included friend, spouse/family, and professor (at 1%). When asked to locate where certain experiences and activities took place, whether inside the seminary or outside it, 56% of the students said that their spiritual development took place outside the seminary. Judging from these results, it seems that the classroom experience ranks third in comparison to the more dominant influence of the church and its leadership. What this study suggests is that students intuitively understand and operate within an ecosystem perspective. What Palka (2004) called "community settings" we are calling an ecosystem, but the concept is the same. He was able to identify from student self-descriptions, various elements of each person's community that had an impact on his or her spiritual development. What should alert us as theological educators is the profound influence of external contexts and settings on our students.

Spiritual formation and education. Theological education can be a vehicle by which a person can be transformed into whole-person formation. Cetuk (1998) addresses this issue in her book, *What to Expect in Seminary: Theological Education as Spiritual Formation.* Her view is that seminary education needs to be approached from the perspective of spiritual formation, not simply intellectual development. It isn't enough to only educate the mind or challenge the body. As educators, we need to take into consideration the whole person in context. Each individual brings to the academy a host of ecosystem components. Our ability to harness those significant elements is part of the proactive and intentional nature of Christian education. The term intentional is used to refer to the responsibility of online educators and students to engage in all aspects of formation, including spiritual, social, and intellectual. This being said, it is understood that the Holy Spirit is the primary motivator or force in achieving growth and maturity in spiritual formation.

Formation is partially achieved through direct engagement by self-directed individuals for the purpose of sharing ideas, values, and experiences with others. Those of us who have been in the classroom could argue that idealized notions of community formation in geographical proximity are just that. I have witnessed students texting, instant-messaging, emailing, Facebooking, and surfing the Internet during a face-to-face class period. Conversely, I have read online discussion board posts of students who reveal personal details in a way that appears to reflect deliberative and intentional thought. These posts have elicited formative moments for both the online community as well as the individuals themselves. The purpose of this chapter is certainly not to elevate one venue of teaching and learning over another but simply to point out that spiritual formation, as an intentional outcome of theological education, happens wherever the Holy Spirit is allowed to function. When we limit the Spirit's work, we delude ourselves and in so doing, hamper growth opportunities.

Developing community-based models for theological distance education requires the realization that technology alone cannot create or maintain human relationships and should not replace them. Furthermore, this approach embraces an ecosystems view of one's contributing community on the learning process. Advances in technology have shaped our ability to build community, both positively and negatively, but the reality is that community building happens despite the limitations some see in various forms of media. The growing body of resources found in pedagogical media is forcing some to rethink previously held notions of limited communication. Much of the same research is changing the way we view embodiment in online communities. Hess (2000) argued that online education is an embodied form of learning. Students interact with the medium of technology through the use of the mental, physical, emotional, and spiritual dimensions.

Similarly, the divide between the individual and community is contrary to an ecological perspective of spiritual formation. Connectedness preceded the existence of individuals and was not created as a result of entities coming together in unity. Rice (2009) makes the point that in order for Adam to be truly complete and whole, a suitable helper was created that would complement the need for connectedness. At the core of human existence lies the need for connection with others. Although God created individual beings with unique particularities, people were not created to be and remain in isolation from others. Using an ecosystems approach helps us understand that online education is not an isolating experience but rather one other form of connectedness.

CONCLUSION

The implications of the ecosystem model for understanding spiritual formation in theological distance education provide us with a tangible model both to assess growth as well as to understand how formation occurs. If student formation empowered by the Holy Spirit takes place in a variety of settings and contexts—some of which involve physical proximity, some of which involve virtual community, and some of which involve individual encounters with texts, images, sounds, and their own mental constructs—then the model that has been proposed enables us to consider all of these as potentially beneficial to student spiritual development. We can no longer focus on one dimension to the exclusion of the others, as indicated by student self-reports in my study. Their understanding (intellectual) of course content facilitated a deeper relationship with God (spiritual) and other students (social). They encouraged one another with examples from their own ministries and to this day, those relationships formed online continue to be as present as those developed in the face-to-face classroom.

DISCUSSION QUESTIONS

1. One model for a personal ecosystem is the hand. The thumb represents the physical dimension, the forefinger represents the intellect, the middle represents the emotional dimension, the ring finger represents the social dimension, the little finger represents the moral dimension, and finally, the palm represents the spiritual dimension. Each of these components of the hand is interrelated as is one's ecosystem. As you look at each of these dimensions, how would you incorporate those elements into your online course?
2. One's connections have direct bearing on learning and development. Identify one other individual with whom you have a relationship and describe specific ways in which that person has produced observable change in you, using the following list.
    -   Behavior
    -   Relationships
    -   Knowledge of scripture
    -   Sociability
    -   Physical condition
    -   Emotional well-being
    -   Values
    -   Spiritual development

3. We know that interaction with others contributes to growth and formation in all aspects of a person's development, including spiritual formation. Based on the following list of reciprocal actions, how would you incorporate these components into an online course?
   - Care for one another
   - Encourage one another
   - Challenge one another
   - Pray for one another
   - Teach one another
   - Forgive one another
   - Edify or build up one another
   - Serve one another

4. One of the ways to diagram one's ecosystem is through an ecoscan. Take a few moments to identify those contexts in your life that impact you, for better or for worse. Draw a circle in the middle of your paper. This circle represents you. From there, draw circles around you representing *primary* contexts and settings in which you live and function as a person (immediate family, church, school, work, civic organizations, groups, friends, etc.). From those circles, add smaller circles that represent *secondary* contexts (church ministries, organizations connected to work, extended family, etc.) Continue adding circles as they relate. Draw thin lines (weak connections) connecting the secondary contexts to the primary ones, dotted lines connecting to sub-groups, and so on.

REFERENCES

Bronfenbrenner, U. (1979). *The ecology of human development.* Cambridge, MA: Harvard University Press.

Cetuk, V. (1998). *What to expect in seminary: Theological education as spiritual formation.* Nashville, TN: Abingdon Press.

Cristakis, N., & Fowler, J. (2009). *Connected: The surprising power of our social networks and how they shape our lives.* New York: Little, Brown and Company.

Fowler, J. W. (1981). *Stages of faith: The psychology of human development and the quest for meaning.* San Francisco: Harper Collins.

Hess, M. E. (2000, November). *Attending to embodiedness in online, theologically focused learning.* Paper presented at Going the Distance: Theology, Religious Education, and Interactive Distance Education, at University of Dayton, Ohio. Retrieved September 4, 2006, from http://www.luthersem.edu/mhess/dayton.pdf

Palka, J. (2004). Defining a theological education community. *International Review of Research in Open and Distance Learning, 5*(3). Retrieved April 22, 2005, from http://www.irrodl.org/index.php/irrodl/article/view/197/279

Rice, J. (2009). *The church of facebook: How the hyperconnected are redefining community.* Colorado Springs, CO: David C. Cook.

Roehlkepartain, E. C., King, P. E., Wagener, L. M., & Benson, P. L. (2006). *The handbook of spiritual development in childhood and adolescence.* Thousand Oaks, CA: Sage.

Ward, T. (1995). Foreword. In J. Wilhoit & J. Dettoni (Eds.), *Nurture that is Christian* (pp. 7–17) Wheaton, IL: Victor Books.

Worster, D. (1998). *Nature's economy: A history of ecological ideas.* Cambridge, NY: Cambridge University Press.

CHAPTER 6

CHALLENGES AND OPPORTUNITIES FOR ONLINE THEOLOGICAL EDUCATION

James Riley Estep Jr.
Lincoln Christian University

Steven Yates
Lancaster Bible College

Within any industry there are always opportunities for innovation, but with those opportunities come related challenges. Online theological education can be seen as a glass half full or half empty, as it presents parallel challenges and opportunities. While research reveals that online and face-to-face courses have no significant difference in student learning, many institutions are still hesitant to provide online courses (U.S. Department of Education, 2009).

What are the unique challenges and opportunities within Christian higher education for online education at seminaries, graduate schools, universities and Bible colleges? What questions may arise concerning a president's or dean's decision to investigate online courses? Each institution has to consider certain decision aspects and how each will impact the institution.

Best Practices of Online Education, pages 65–77

The purpose of this chapter is *not* to provide prescriptions for every challenge presented by online education in Christian higher education (as a matter of fact, this is the purpose of the whole book). Rather, it is designed to provide the terrain of the online education debate—the shadowy valleys and mountaintop experiences—so as to better prepare a faculty member or administrator in introducing and implementing an online education strategy. The chapter will address these challenges and opportunities within four dimensions: Institutional, Faculty, Students, and Constituency. Decision makers need appropriate information to guide investments of limited institutional funds. They need to see that the best way to overcome challenges is to override them with opportunities and determine if the benefits of online education outweigh the risk.

INSTITUTIONAL CHALLENGES AND OPPORTUNITIES

Christian higher education is at a crossroads between maintaining traditional campus culture and adapting or integrating alternative delivery systems. The stakeholders are challenged with issues of funding, accrediting, staffing, student demand, and philosophy.

According to a study by the National Center for Education Statistics (NCES), student enrollment for ages 25–34 will increase 28% between 2008 and 2019, while enrollment for ages 35 and older will increase 22% during the same period (Hussar & Bailey, 2011). This trend provides both the opportunity to grow by attracting an expanding adult student population, and the challenge of meeting them where they live and work. An institution has to evaluate its mission and vision to ensure alignment with new alternative delivery systems that fit the institution.

Mission/Vision

"*Where are we headed now?*" When the conversation of online learning or alternative delivery systems begins, constituents begin to ask, "Are we even supposed to be considering this? Is this really the kind of thing our institution should do? Will we be able to shift our professors online? Is it too late?" Executive committee level evaluation must take place to assess the readiness of the institution to adapt to online Christian education. Is the institution capable of providing online classes?

Each institution has to determine the level of online course integration. The number of courses could be determined by accreditation standards, available technology systems, institutional philosophy, or faculty willing to convert courses. The president and executive staff may consider an internal study or discussion forums to determine if online courses are a match with the institution's mission and vision. A consultant could analyze the existing structures, meet with faculty and staff, and provide details of opportunities and challenges for the institution. The final decision can be communicated through a new vision statement, a press release, a newsletter, or a presidential letter.

Some questions to consider: (a) Should we offer a fully online degree? (b) Does a fully online degree meet our accreditation standards? (c) Should we offer online certificates? (d) Where do we think the students are coming from? (e) How much online implementation should we consider? (f) What is an appropriate timeline? (g) Who needs to be involved in the decisions?

Institutional/Administrative

"How do we get there?" Once an institution has determined that online education meets its mission, the institution has to determine the level of online course integration. The number of courses could be determined by accreditation standards (fully online degree vs. hybrid/blended degree), available technology systems, institutional philosophy, or faculty willingness to convert courses.

Some other areas to consider are: (a) Encouraging faculty participation—How do we get them onboard? (b) Determining new courses—What should we teach? (c) Researching new markets—Where will students come from? (d) Examining course creation process—Did we get it right? (e) Measuring and evaluating courses—What did they learn? (f) Surveying faculty feedback—Are they with us? (g) Aligning online courses with existing semester schedule or making them open "jump in and jump out" schedules—How much flexibility for students? (Yates, 2009).

Technological

"Campus I.T. can't even keep projectors running; how are we even equipped to do online education?" Using the appropriate technology can be a daunting task. Online and hybrid courses require certain technology pieces and staff members. Some dean technology considerations: (a) Do you have an adequate delivery system? (b) What type of support staff and help desk is available for faculty and students? (c) Who will maintain your systems? (d) Will your system be onsite or hosted? (e) How will faculty be trained?

Steve Delamarter (2006) lists three kinds of failures organizations may experience when implementing new technology into existing programs: (a) failing completely to see the potential and impact of a new technology; (b) responding inadequately and belatedly to the challenge of the use of technology by a competitor; and (c) underutilizing a new technology by forcing it into the constraints of an old model of understanding (Delamarter, 2006).

Financial

"Who's going to pay for this?" Many institutions perceive online courses as a hidden revenue stream that will save the organization. Few reports include the total costs of operation including initial and ongoing operational costs. A few financial considerations are: (a) initial cost of hardware, software, and installation; (b) staff payroll, contractors, and service contracts; (c) public opinion of institution; (d) potential gain or loss of students; (e) institutional image and impact on donors; (f) faculty training and development; (g) initial course conversion; (h) initial marketing and image costs; and (i) Cost of staying the same—Can we afford not to change?

Deans can use a cost comparison tool to evaluate the costing differences between two delivery systems such as a training cost return on investment spreadsheet (Excel Templates, 2011). Real and estimated expenses can be entered and compared. The results could have a considerable impact on the funding and timing of an institution's conversion to online courses.

The next section will review faculty challenges and opportunities to online Christian higher education. What should be expected of faculty? How will they respond? What institutional support should be provided? These and other questions will be answered.

FACULTY CHALLENGES AND OPPORTUNITIES

Institutions are realizing the necessity to implement blended and online courses and need the faculty to participate by learning a new delivery system. Kaye Shelton and George Saltsman (2005) state, "because online education is a new paradigm, many faculty are unprepared for the fundamental differences in the roles required for online teaching. The lack of preparation necessitates a higher level of involvement by administrators to ensure success" (p. 59). The institution's future sustainability may be directly linked to the faculty openly embracing this new delivery system.

Jane Cole and Jeffrey Kritzer (2009) mention that "the increase of online course offerings has been a challenge to faculty. A combination of factors have created this challenge: (a) the pressure on universities to create online/hybrid programs in a short amount of time, (b) lack of access to technological resources in a timely fashion, and (c) lack of adequate instructor training on the implementation of effective online instruction" (Cole & Kritzer, 2009, p. 37).

Accepting a New Delivery System

"You want me to do what?" Faculty may be learning a new delivery system that involves complex technology systems. Judith Boettcher and Rita-Marie Conrad (2010) expound, "Many faculty find themselves in this state of concern and trepidation when they agree to teach a course online. Just minutes later, they often wonder what they have agreed to do and can feel clueless about what the first step might be" (p. 388). The institution has to provide a clear path of training and support to ensure the faculty they are not alone.

Another challenge for faculty is understanding the intrinsic and extrinsic rewards for learning and excelling with the new delivery system. Faculty may view the new system as a negative investment of time. The dean or department chair needs to express the faculty recognition, the value to the institution, and the personal satisfaction of learning a new system.

Receiving Adequate Training and Development

"I'm a dinosaur when it comes to technology! I'm lost . . . just how do you teach what I teach online?" A decision-maker needs to evaluate the training possibilities and determine which ones are cost effective, functional, and fit the current academic environment. Steve Yates (2009) lists eight types of faculty development for alternative delivery systems: (a) consultant or help desk—answer pedagogical and technical questions when professors are in need; (b) initial training—boot camp or one day required class; (c) on demand or ongoing training or workshop—variety of classes to build on initial training; (d) mandatory training course(s)—required classes before creating a course and/or before teaching the first time; (e) conference— encourage better pedagogical skills and help faculty see the connection between pedagogy and technology; (f) optional training course(s)—regularly scheduled development courses; (g) special guest speaker(s)—address pedagogical, technical, or industry changes impacting institutions' alternative delivery systems; and (h) training web site—teaching and preparation tools. Jane Cole and Jeffrey Kritzer (2009) state:

> The prospect of having to learn to teach new courses in an online environment can be intimidating and stressful for faculty members who are new to higher education. They not only must become experts in the content of the particular courses but also must become proficient using the hardware and software needed to effectively teach online classes. (p. 36)

Training and development courses can be created by internal staff, purchased through contract with organizations like Sloan Consortium, or completed through certification processes. Each institution has to determine their level of internal expertise, timing, and budget for faculty development of alternative delivery systems.

Understanding Faculty Incentives

"What's in it for me?" Faculty are searching for credibility, internal and external opportunities for recognition, paths to promotion, and incentives to try new teaching methods or alternative delivery systems. Yates (2009) discovered a number of faculty incentives to adapt alternative delivery systems: (a) individual preparedness—personal desire to develop skills with alternative delivery systems; (b) faculty peer pressure—curiosity and buzz created by new ideas; (c) hands on experience—lab type of environment rather than just a lecture; (d) faculty peer recognition—publicly sharing what the faculty has accomplished; (e) discovering new things together—opportunity to learn new features together; (f) faculty's seeing the value of faculty development—interacting with fellow professors; and (g) recovery of class time—move to online discussion.

Providing Program Improvements

Faculty members are mostly open to change when they can realize a benefit or improvement to the existing programs. A decision maker could select one or more of the following program improvements to consider implementing at their institution (Yates, 2009): (a) adding course enhancing software applications; (b) evaluating and reorganizing existing training; (c) impacting faculty portfolio and tenure; (d) providing articles and information; (e) providing ADS course of semester award; (f) adding audio conference training platform; (g) providing food with training; and (h) adding webinar or Skype interactive training platform.

The dean has to ensure the faculty understand the change and could use a faculty focus group to evaluate and rank the above eight programs improvement options to assimilate the faculty into the change process. The faculty members can own the change process and willingly implement the program improvements that will help them and improve the overall student experience.

STUDENT CHALLENGES AND OPPORTUNITIES

It is safe to assume that our students are more tech savvy than we are, and that they are more comfortable around the revolving door of technological innovations. This generation(s) grew up with laptops, wireless internet, and smart phones and are the early adopters of technological innovation. However, when it comes to distance education via online classrooms, their reactions may not be so enthusiastic. Student challenges and opportunities abound in Christian higher education's online venture.

Building Online Learning Communities

"Somehow I thought my college experience would be more like a classroom than a chat room." Institutions of higher education are *learning communities*. Learning is not limited to the individual endeavors of a siloed student, but is a communal act taking place in the library, class discussions and activities, and even more so outside the classroom. *How does online education create community?* Creating community in online learning environments is *challenging* for several reasons, but they all center on the absence of physical proximity, in other words, students and instructors are not in a physical classroom or on a physical campus when engaged in online education. While some assess this as an insurmountable obstacle to providing theological education online, numerous studies have indicated that a real sense of community can be formed through an online learning format (Esselman, 2004; Shore, 2007; Silvers, O'Connell, & Ferrell, 2007; Tyron & Bishop, 2009). Physical proximity is not a requirement for authentic Christian community, as Paul wrote to the Colossian congregation, "For though I am absent from you in body, I am present with you in spirit and delight to see how orderly you are and how firm your faith in Christ is" (Col. 2:5 New International Version).

Community is a naturally occurring quality facilitated by common shared experiences and can be readily achieved in on online learning environment. Several pedagogical elements contribute significantly to providing online theological students a stimulus for community formation (cf. Heinemann, 2005a, 2005b, 2006, 2007), focusing on students' mental presence rather than physical presence. For example, some institutions utilize long-term cohorts to form community, wherein students become familiar not only with one another's ideas and convictions, but with one another's background, life situation, pastoral vision, and personal lives. Similarly, online pedagogy tends to avoid a content focus, emphasizing a more constructivist approach to theological education, requiring significant interaction between students and the instructor, as well as dialog between the students as genuine colleagues in the learning process.

Community can also be built *beyond* the online classroom. Just as dorms, coffee houses, and special events provide co-curricular communal opportunities, parallel provisions can be made online. Some institutions have dedicated chat-rooms to provide students in their university or seminary a place to interact, giving it a name like eCafé, an online student union. Adding a prayer blog or even discussion board for podcasted chapel services provides a venue to students to interact with one another beyond the course cohort. Including online students in the routine information services of the campus, such as newsletters or even alumni mailings likewise builds a sense of belonging and acceptance by the campus community. Perhaps one of the greatest opportunities online education affords theological education is an actual global community; students gathered from throughout the world while remaining in their own culture and ministry settings, sharing together in theological and pastoral dialog. Ultimately, community building is the responsibility of the students. They determine whether to remain isolated or to engage in the campus community, even when that campus is digital.

Facilitating Spiritual Formation

"I didn't know the internet was spiritual?" Education that is Christian is concerned with more than the mastery of subject matter and skilled performance. As Christians, faculty members see the students as more than people, but as individuals made in God's image and having a relationship with Him. For Christian higher education, *spiritual formation* of our students is not an optional; it is a distinctive mark of the educational experience, part of the institutional DNA. This is born out of our heritage as Christian institutions, our denominational affiliations, theological traditions, and even pastoral conviction. This is such a crucial matter, that the Association for Biblical Higher Education (ABHE Standard 8) and the Association of Theological Schools (ATS Degree Standards 4.1; 5.1) actually require institutions to document and assess their commitment to providing for the spiritual formation of students, even in online learning environments.

Attending to the spiritual formation of student indeed presents unique challenges to online Christian higher education. Similar to the community formation concerns, spiritual formation must navigate through the challenge of nurturing and facilitating students spirituality in an online learning environment. Mark Maddix (Maddix & Estep, 2010), Dean of the Theology at Northwest Nazarene University (Nappa, Idaho) suggests a three-fold approach to facilitating spiritual formation in online theological education (Figure 6.1, adapted).

In summary, whatever can be provided to promote the spiritual formation of students in an on-campus educational venue can in fact be paralleled in an online learning venue, with relatively the same assurance of having a positive impact. Online learning communities are a context of untapped potential for Christian nurture. It is an opportunity to share with one another our common faith in Christ Jesus around the virtual table,

Inward Domain	Outward Domain	Corporate Domain
This domain centers on the internal righteousness of the person and typically involves disciplines like meditation, prayer, fasting, and study.	This domain focuses on the person's call to discover the social implications of simplicity, submission, and service.	This domain helps people explore the disciplines of confession, worship, guidance, and celebration as members of a community of faith.
Spiritual Practices:	*Spiritual Practices:*	*Spiritual Practices:*
• Prayer blogs/requests • Scripture Reading • Iconography • Devotional Literature • Journaling (transparency) • Rituals	• Chapel podcast with interactive blog for application • Integrated spiritual assignments included in each online course	• Relationship/Community • Online Community Chat Room for Students • Spiritual Direction/ Mentor

Figure 6.1 Domains of spiritual formation.

creating a community that nurtures and facilitates our growth in Christ and with one another.

Insuring Academic Integrity

Test peeking, plagiarism, falsifying work, even identity theft… it's hard enough to catch students engaged in such activities in the classroom or even on campus, let alone in an online course. "Online! They'll never know it isn't me doing the work." One prevalent student challenge of online higher education is insuring the academic integrity of the student and the program. However, insuring this is no greater challenge for online students as compared to on-campus students. A student can submit a plagiarized or falsified papers in class as easily as online. Online testing can be done by e-proctor, or a camera that allows the student to be observed while taking a test. Similarly, the same mechanisms in place for confirming the identity of an on-campus student can be modified slightly to accommodate online students, with the same level of assurance that the student is in fact the person they report to be. In short, the challenges posed by online students is no more significant that those posed by students in on campus programs. The basic response to the issue is to provide a well articulated, comprehensive statement of standards of conduct for online education, describing and defining each facet of academic integrity, with the potential penalties a student may face if the standards of conduct are violated (cf. Kitahara & Westfall, 2007). Also, compliance with the latest edition of "Best Practices for Electronically Delivered Degree and Certificate Programs" (Instructional Technology Council, 2011) will provide insights to insuring academic integrity.

CONSTITUENCY CHALLENGES AND OPPORTUNITIES

Constituencies are unique to each institution of Christian higher education. Alumni, congregations, denominational bodies, peer institution, even the parents of undergraduate students in a Bible college or Christian university cumulatively comprise the constituency of our respective institutions. Each administration weights the elements within the institution's constituency, assessing how much "voice" they have in the decision making and direction for the institution, including a venture into online education.

Alumni Reactions

By their very nature, loyal alumni are reminiscent about their alma mater. They will recall with fondness dorm life, relationships with peers, the mentoring of a special faculty member, chapel services, or small groups. Alumni may perceive online education to lack the distinctive character of the education they experienced at their institution. Of course, the opportunity provided by online education is to broaden the institution's educational outreach beyond the confines of the campus, having a direct global impact on the Church and world. Still, attention should be given to include within the online program the elements distinct to the university's curriculum. Core courses that are distinctive to the institution, utilizing leading faculty members, introducing online students to key campus communicators, as well as orienting them not only to the mechanics of the online program, but introducing new students to the heritage and legacy of the institution will achieve this. Students need to feel connected not only to the cohort, but also to the campus they will one day call their alma mater.

Ordination...Online?

"You don't learn about ministry through megapixels!" Accreditation bodies struggle with the affirmation of distance theological education because many denominational bodies struggle with the idea of ordaining candidates who never "attended" a Bible college or seminary, in other words did not experience pastoral training as did past generations. Similar to the alumni reaction, those responsible for overseeing the process of ordination, whether that is through a congregation or denominational entity, wrestle with assessing the preparatory value of online pastoral training. Will online pastoral students meet the qualifications for ordination? Will they be acceptable to denomination or tradition with which the institution is affiliated? Will they be "marketable" in comparison with other pastoral

candidates considered for an open position? These questions should be addressed by the institution prior to entering into an online program of theological education. One major opportunity it does provide is for the equipping of pastors in the global Christian community, those who are perhaps remote from a Christian university or seminary. Online education makes theological education more accessible to more individuals globally than in any previous generation.

Collegial Perceptions

"What will others think of us?" No institution is an island. We are part of an academic community. Even accreditation bodies rely not only on standards, but upon the process of "peer review," or members of the academic community holding one another accountable. What will our peers think of an online degree from our institution? Will it be regarded sub-standard, competitive, or marketable? First, new technologies have always been incorporated into higher education with a predictable level of skepticism and passive resistance. Any technological innovation spells *change* for faculty, curriculum, administration, and to an extent the institution as a whole; and that is not always welcome. Second, the real concern is maintaining the academic integrity within the higher education community regardless of the program being offered. To guide institutions into the age of digital learning, the eight major accreditation agencies in the United States have developed a set of *best practices* "in response to the emergence of technologically mediated instruction offered at a distance as an important component of higher education" (Instructional Technology Council, 2011, p. 1). This document supplies reasonable expectations for institutions to guarantee that quality instruction is provided through online education. It assures a degree of similarity among accredited institutions that engage in online education. Our institutional constituents agree on the standards for providing online quality Christian higher education.

CONCLUSION

Each institution has to ponder the value, cost, and philosophical fit of implementing online education. Does this new delivery method meet our mission and vision, excite our faculty, equip our students, and maintain positive relationships with all constituents? The primary challenge in changing to online education delivery is often wrongly identified as technology only. Multiple institutional components have to be reviewed as to the impact on each other. A decision-maker has to ensure sustainability and not waste limited resources on a delivery vehicle that would never effectively function at the institution. In the end, the opportunities must outweigh the challenges; the benefit must be greater than the risk.

DISCUSSION QUESTIONS

1. Given the list of challenges provided above, what are the top two challenges your institution faces when engaging in distance education online?
2. Similarly, what are the two greatest opportunities that distance education online can aid your institution to achieve its mission?
3. Can you itemize three to four changes that would start moving from challenges to opportunities in distance education online? List them.

REFERENCES

Boettcher, J., & Conrad, R. (2010). *The online teaching survival guide: Simple and practical pedagogical tips.* San Francisco: Jossey-Bass.

Cole, J., & Kritzer, J. (2009). Strategies for success: Teaching an online course. *Rural Special Education Quarterly, 28*(4), 36–40.

Delamarter, S. (2006). Strategic planning to enhance teaching and learning with technology. *Teaching Theology and Religion, 9*(1), 9–23.

Excel Templates. (2011). *Training costs and ROI calculator.* Retrieved April 6, 2011, from http://exceltemplates.net/financial/roi/training-cost-and-roi-calculator/

Esselman, T. (2004). The pedagogy of the online wisdom community: Forming church ministers in a digital age. *Teaching Theology and Religion, 7*(3), 159–170.

Heinemann, M. H. (2005a). Teacher-student interaction and learning in on-line theological education, Part I: Concepts and concerns. *Christian Higher Education, 4*, 183–209.

Heinemann, M. H. (2005b). Teacher-student interaction and learning in on-line theological education, Part II: Additional theoretical frameworks. *Christian Higher Education, 4*, 277–297.

Heinemann, M. H. (2006). Teacher-student interaction and learning in on-line theological education, Part III: Methodological approach. *Christian Higher Education, 5*, 161–182.

Heinemann, M. H. (2007). Teacher-student interaction and learning in on-line theological education, Part IV: Findings and conclusions. *Christian Higher Education, 6*, 185–206.

Hussar, W., & Bailey, T. (2011). *Projections of education statistics to 2019.* National Center for Education Statistics. Retrieved March 16, 2011, from http://nces.ed.gov/pubsearch/pubsinfo.asp?pubid=2011017

Instructional Technology Council. (2011). *Best Practices for Electronically Offered Degree and Certificate Programs.* Washington, DC: Author. Retrieved from http://www.itcnetwork.org/resources/articles-abstracts-and-research/356-best-practices-for-electronically-offered-degree-and-certificate-programs.html?catid=48%3Alibrary-articles-abstracts-research

Kitahara, R. T., & Westfall, F. (2007). Promoting academic integrity in online distance learning courses. *Journal of Online Learning and Teaching, 3*(3). Retrieved October 1, 2011, from http://jolt.merlot.org/vol3no3/kitahara.htm

Maddix, M. A. & Estep, J. R. (2010). Spiritual formation in online higher education communities: Nurturing spirituality in Christian higher education online degree programs. *Christian Education Journal, Series 3, 7*(2), 423–436.

Shelton, K. & Saltsman, G. (2005). *An administrator's guide to online education.* Charlotte, NC: Information Age Publishing.

Shore, M. H. (2007). Establishing social presence in online courses: Why and how. *Theological Education, 42*(2), 91–100.

Silvers, P., O'Connell, J., & Fewell, M. (2007). Strategies for creating community in graduate education online programs. *Journal of Computing in Teacher Education, 23*(3), 81–87.

Tyron, P. J. & Bishop, M. J. (2009). Theoretical foundations for enhancing social connectedness in online learning environments. *Distance Education, 30*(3), 291–315.

U.S. Department of Education. (2009). *Evaluation of evidence-based practices in online learning: A meta-analysis and review of online learning studies.* Retrieved June 10, 2011, from http://www2.ed.gov/rschstat/eval/tech/evidence-based-practices/finalreport.pdf

Yates, S. (2009). *Current faculty development practices for alternative delivery systems in Christian higher education institutions: A qualitative study* (Unpublished doctoral dissertation). The Southern Baptist Theological Seminary, Louisville, KY.

SECTION II

GENERATING AND FACILITATING EFFECTIVE LEARNING IN ONLINE EDUCATION

CHAPTER 7

BEST PRACTICES IN ONLINE TEACHING

C. Damon Osborne
Mount Vernon Nazarene University

INTRODUCTION

When first considering possible "best practices" for teaching in the online learning environment, it is easy to merely modify practices and materials from existing face-to-face teaching experiences. However, the differences between the online learning environment and the traditional face-to-face classroom require that online instructors take a different approach when developing an online teaching practice (Swan, 2010). This is not to say that sound teaching and learning principles cannot bridge the gap between online and traditional delivery methods; instead, it is important to identify the differences between the two and develop strategies that facilitate effective learning.

This chapter provides guidelines to developing effective learning in an online environment, which include preparing the course prior to teaching the course, establishing social presence in the online course, facilitating effectively, maintaining boundaries between online work and life, and bringing closure to an online course. These best practices provide the online teacher with techniques to effective online teaching.

Best Practices of Online Education, pages 81–90
Copyright © 2012 by Information Age Publishing
All rights of reproduction in any form reserved.

PREPARE THE COURSE

To those who have engaged in an online educational venture, it is not at all surprising that some of the best teaching in the online setting takes place before the student is enrolled in the course. Although some traditional educators may feel a conflict between their academic independence and the need for course materials to be ready prior to the start of the course (Haughey, 2010), there are valid reasons for this process. Consider this contrast between the traditional face-to-face classroom and the online learning environment. On the first day of a traditional face-to-face the instructor and the students generally spend significant time covering the contents of the syllabus, the expectations of the instructor, and any initial student questions about the course. Conversely, the students in an online course are generally presented with a web page in a learning management system.

Therefore, the first impression a student receives from an online course is directly related to the preparation that takes place prior to making the course available to students. Although some design and construction considerations are outside the control of the instructor (the theme/design of the learning management system employed, or the way the students' browsers display the online materials), the actual course materials directly developed by the instructor must be presented in a manner that encourages the students to engage with the course content and with the instructor. Consider the following terms when preparing to develop an online course: comprehensive, concise, clear, and connected.

The online instructor may not have the opportunity to share the expectations of the course synchronously, as instructors in face-to-face courses, which makes it is necessary that all information presented in an online class be comprehensive in nature. Carefully consider any possible questions when developing all of the course materials, not merely the syllabus, so that confusion is avoided at the outset of the course (Crews, Wilkinson, Hemby, McCannon, & Wiedmaier, 2008). Many online students want to take in a comprehensive overview of a course from the very beginning, requiring the online instructor to fully develop the course ahead of time.

However, the balance to the comprehensive view of course development is the concept of remaining as concise as possible when authoring materials. This may appear contradictory at first, but the key is that the instructor should provide instructions in such a manner as to comprehensively address the task at hand without unnecessary information. In other words, provide all of the requisite information and nothing more.

The concept of clarity not only applies to the development of course materials (i.e., language usage, instructions, etc.), but also to the layout of the course. Since the online instructor is constrained by the limitations of the learning management system, appropriate labeling of resources and assignments affords the student an easier path of navigation when entering unfamiliar territory. Nearly everyone is familiar with the general layout of a typical school building, which includes finding the front door to the building, the main office, the classrooms, and restrooms. However, the concept of landmarks taken for granted in the face-to-face environment translates to confused students in the online learning environment when it is not clear where the assignments are to be submitted, or when discussion posts are due (Crews et al., 2008). Coupling this concept of clarity with an earlier thought leads to the conclusion that all online course materials need to be as clear as they are comprehensive.

Finally, when preparing an online course for delivery, the instructor must make sure that the appropriate connections are in place. As with many terms, the word connected has two meanings in this context: connections in the course materials and connections between the course participants. The instructor ensures that the materials of the course are connected appropriately, which means that all tools function as intended. Online courses tend to use resources such as websites, resources that can appear to be ephemeral in nature. Therefore, inspecting all links prior to going live is imperative for the online instructor. Additionally, many courses are constructed using learning outcomes or objectives derived from a set of standards. Just as it is important to check the web links present in the course for accuracy, it is also necessary to review the course materials from the perspective of the learning outcomes. In other words, ensure that the course actually presents content that helps the students reach the intended outcomes. Finally, the construction of course materials, such as open-ended questions for discussion, should allow the course participants the opportunity to connect with one another and the course content.

ESTABLISHING SOCIAL PRESENCE

Once the course has been fully developed and checked for accuracy by the instructor, the teaching aspect of the course begins. Of primary importance is the establishment of social presence on the part of the online instructor (Moallem, 2007). In the context of an online course, the concept of social presence refers to the perception of the instructor as an actual human being, in addition to his or her role as an active and engaged participant in the course. Just as students in a face-to-face setting take their social cues from the instructor at the front of the room, online students also seek guidance from the instructor on how to interact in a classroom where they may never see one another physically. There are two interconnected means of addressing the issue of social presence in an online classroom: *tools* and *techniques*. Although the tools discussed below are common to nearly every learning management system (or in the possession of individual course participants), it is the specific techniques employed that allow the instructor the ability to establish his or her social presence in the online classroom.

The heart of online learning is the threaded discussion board. This tool is widely used in courses where social discussion leads to the construction of a knowledge base among the students (Hurst, Camp & Hall, 2009). However, it is also an excellent tool for the instructor to use when attempting to establish social presence. At the outset of an online course, the discussion board can be used to introduce the instructor to the class (Dennen, 2007). This is an excellent opportunity for the students to hear the instructor's voice in writing, providing them insight into the instructor as a person. When considering what types of information to provide in this written introduction, the instructor should not be afraid to let his or her personality shine. In a face-to-face setting there are many cues (including non-verbal cues) that help students understand the perspective of the instructor. However, in the online setting, which is primarily text-based, meaning can be harder to ascertain without carefully crafted messages from the instructor. Therefore, an introduction that pairs a section on professional experience with a section that anecdotally tells the story of a given nickname humanizes the instructor in an environment that can appear to be cold or detached to many students.

While a verbal introduction is an absolute requirement in developing social presence in an online classroom, the use of video in conjunction with the introduction further enhances the cues that the online students receive at the outset of the course. For those instructors who might be intimidated when considering how to incorporate a video into their online course , it should be noted that there are a number of increasingly easy to use tools to make such a task far simpler than it has been in the past.

Before delving into a video upload workflow, the primary consideration should be the content to be filmed. Again, this is a prime opportunity for the instructor's personality to be presented to the online students, so consider that when crafting the message. A word of caution on the use of video: keep the video brief, particularly in the case of the "talking head." Although some instructors are comfortable speaking extemporaneously, many need to script out their video entirely. Neither approach is incorrect, provided that the instructor practices enough with the filming process to appear comfortable and relaxed on video. The introductory video could include a brief introduction to the course, a formal introduction from the instructor, and a personal story from the instructor.

As for the actual creation of the video, the following steps are involved: planning, filming, editing, hosting, and then sharing. As the planning of the video was discussed previously, the next step in the process to explore is filming (or, perhaps more accurately, recording). Keep in mind that an elaborate video setup is not required for this purpose. In fact, the webcam that is built into the bezel of many laptops is perfectly suited for recording. Additionally, video cameras, cell phones, and even many still cameras can provide the necessary video capture for this project. Once the video segment has been captured, it needs to be imported to a computer for editing and/or uploading to a video hosting site. There are free (and relatively easy to use) video editing tools for both the Windows and Mac OS X platforms. Upon the completion of the editing process, uploading the video to a hosting site (e.g., YouTube) will allow the instructor the ability to later link to, or directly embed, the video in a learning management system.

The introductory video coupled with a discussion post only establishes the social presence of the online instructor. In order to truly breathe life into the online course, and maintain that social presence throughout, the online instructor must facilitate the online course effectively.

FACILITATION

Facilitating an online course is different than teaching in a face-to-face setting. This role must be undertaken with both "rigor and attention" (Norton & Hathaway, 2008, p. 489) in order to fully engage online students. Many instructors, particularly those without knowledge of educational theory, are most comfortable teaching how they were taught, through lecture and testing (Marek, 2009). In an online classroom, however, there are some significant challenges in maintaining these past practices. First, if an instructor intended to present content primarily through lecture, he or she would either need to have all course participants online at the same time for a synchronous event or to record the lecture for later viewing (asynchronously). However, both methods present significant challenges in online instruction. One challenge is students seek out online courses is for the convenience of learning on their own schedule, making required synchronous events a hindrance. Also, while posting recorded lectures may appear to be the next logical step to an instructor most accustomed to delivering content via this instructional method, online students may be resistant to sitting and viewing (or merely listening to) prerecorded lectures of any substantial length. If there is material that absolutely must be delivered via lecture, the instructor should chunk this material so that the online students' exposure to this type of content delivery is limited in both time as well as frequency.

Instead of lecturing, the online instructor would be better served to help students make a connection to the course content, assisting them in constructing their own knowledge base from the materials present in the course. A phrase that has worked its way into the vernacular of online education speaks to the need that online instructors must transition from *being the sage on the stage, to being the guide on the side.* While this will look different depending on the course and the instructor, the following framework should provide guidance on developing a facilitation practice as an online instructor: establish social presence, be "Goldilocks" in the discussion forums, and provide timely feedback. The concept of establishing social presence by the instructor was discussed extensively in the prior section, while this section outlines the "Goldilocks" method of interacting in the discussion forums of an online course and the need for timely feedback.

While some online instructors may feel compelled to respond to each and every discussion post made by the students, others choose to stay out of the way entirely in order to allow the students the opportunity to completely drive the discussion. However, the best practice actually lies in the middle ground between these two extremes. Dennen (2007) finds that effective online instructors are able to switch between various positions (i.e., dominant or background) in an online discussion. In a faculty-training course taught by the author, prospective online instructors are exposed to this concept in the first week. There are two required discussion questions for the course participants, and the interaction in each is vastly different. In the first question, the course instructor responds to every post, while in the second, the course instructor only responds when directly addressed by the course participants. At the end of the week, the participants are asked to reflect on these two models of interaction. Most relate that when the instructor replies to everything, it is difficult to find room to participate. Conversely, when there is no presence by the instructor in a question, participants often report that they are hesitant to delve much deeper beyond their initial response in fear they are not moving along the right track. The course instructor then reveals the rule in the weekly feedback, explaining to the participants that neither method of interaction is optimal. Instead, a more balanced (hence "Goldilocks"—not too much, but not too little) approach to interaction is called for to foster in-depth discussion. Online instructors need to be visible in the online course, offering encouragement or redirecting students when the thread of discussion strays from the intended outcomes. Additionally, if there are students who are not being engaged by their peers, the instructor may need to step in and respond in order to commence discussion on their post. Essentially, the instructor should be present enough to keep things moving, without stifling discussion.

One opportunity for the online instructor to add considerable substance to an online course is through timely feedback. Feedback can take place on two levels: *individual and course-wide.* In a face-to-face setting, students have the opportunity to ask questions and have them answered immediately. In the online classroom, however, individual questions often arrive via email, or perhaps on a discussion forum dedicated to questions for the instructor. If the instructor is not present in the class on a regular basis, days could transpire between the time the question is asked and subsequently answered. This merely underscores the need for online instructors to be in the online course on a regular basis, or to experiment with synchronous tools such as instant messaging (Wang & Morgan, 2008), for more immediate responses. Many institutions even provide guidelines or requirements that prescribe how often an instructor must check into their online course. While this will be covered more extensively in the next section, it is indeed important to maintain regular presence in the course.

In addition to responding to individual needs, the online instructor can also provide feedback to the class as a whole at the end of an instructional week (Ko & Rossen, 2004). This feedback can serve a number of purposes: maintaining social presence, facilitating the connection to the content, and simply answering questions. In addition to using video to introduce the instructor to the course participants, video could also be used as part of the weekly feedback. Weekly feedback is delivered through text and video. The text is largely comprised of a summary of the points raised by the students, followed by thoughts and directions to explore from the instructor. The video, on the other hand, is a very brief (generally under two minutes) "talking head" video where the instructor relates the content discussed this week to his teaching practice, or personal life. This is an excellent opportunity to bring the content discussed in forums to life through the use of facial expressions and tone of voice. The online students have the added benefit of hearing the thoughts of their instructor *in the instructor's voice.*

MAINTAIN BOUNDARIES

Although the prior section discussed the need for the instructor to check into an online course on a regular basis, there is a difference between maintaining presence and overworking. Beginning online instructors often find themselves seeking balance between responding in a timely manner and having a life outside of the course. Instead of checking into an online course several times per day, construct a schedule for course work and stick to it (Crews et al., 2008). How an individual instructor's schedule is constructed is dependent upon the number of online courses taught, as well as what other responsibilities the instructor may have (i.e., committee work, thesis advising, etc.).

The caution is that if the instructor sets a precedent by responding immediately to inquiries sent by students in the middle of the night, there will then be an expectation that such immediate responses are standard operating procedure. By establishing a regular schedule of working in an online course at least once per day, five days per week, the online instructor can establish boundaries regarding availability for synchronous communication. In addition to the patterns that students will observe for themselves, it is also useful for the instructor to post information regarding his or her availability in the online course (Smith, 2008). Just as face-to-face instructors provide office hours for their students, so can the online instructors. The key is to be available enough to meet the online students' needs, while also maintaining boundaries with availability so that life and work outside of the online class can continue.

PROVIDE CLOSURE

Finally, when teaching an online course, it is necessary to bring effective closure to the course. Continuing the comparison to the face-to-face environment, on the last day of class, all course participants are certainly aware that they do not need to show up for the course again! However, even when the participants are aware of the start and end dates of the course, the conclusion of an online course should be an intentional event on the part of the instructor.

As the course nears the conclusion, the instructor should begin to bring things to a close by reminding students of any final projects or assessments that need to be submitted. Just as the instructor has been encouraging the online course participants throughout, as the end nears, it is even more important to extend a word of encouragement to those students who appear to be struggling in meeting the demands of the course. This input from the instructor could be just the compassionate motivation that the online student needs to overcome any final obstacles in the course. Finally, it is important to provide final closure for a course by informing the online students when their final grades have been submitted, or at least when they have met the requirements for the course. Again, in an environment that does not have the same generally agreed upon cues that most students are comfortable with from the face-to-face environment, it is essential that the online instructor is explicit when the course begins and ends. Just as it is essential to start the class with an introduction, the online instructor needs to conclude the course intentionally as well.

CONCLUSION

The best online practices provide a core set of principles for developing an online teaching experience. While technology will continue to develop and change, the key to good teaching will always remain the same by engaging students in the process of learning and the pursuit of greater knowledge. This can take place as the instructor is present in the learning context and allows students to discuss the course content. How the instructor facilitates this process determines the effectiveness of an online course.

DISCUSSION QUESTIONS

1. As a new online instructor, what types of challenges might you face if the course was not adequately prepared prior to enrolling students? How might you overcome those challenges?
2. In what ways do instructors establish social presence in an online course? What tools and techniques could be employed to help students connect with the instructor before and during an online course?
3. Describe a plan for effectively facilitating an online discussion. How often will you post in the forum? What types of replies will you provide to students?
4. Reflect upon your current teaching practice, whether online or face-to-face, and consider this question: are there clearly defined boundaries between your personal life and work? In what ways would you establish these boundaries? Outline such a plan.

REFERENCES

Crews, T., Wilkinson, K., Hemby, K. V., McCannon, M., & Wiedmaier, C. (2008). Workload management strategies for online educators. *Delta Pi Epsilon Journal, 50*(3), 132–149.

Dennen, V. P. (2007). Presence and positioning as components of online instructor persona. *Journal of Research on Technology in Education, 40*(1), 95–108.

Haughey, M. (2010). Teaching and learning in distance education before the digital age. In M. F. Cleveland-Innes & D. R. Garrison (Eds.), *An introduction to distance education: Understanding teaching and learning in a new era* (pp. 46–66). New York: Routledge.

Hurst, B., Camp, D., & Hall, C. (2009). Logging in for stronger connections with students: Insights about graduate online teaching. *Journal of Reading Education, 34*(2), 34–37.

Ko, S., & Rossen, S. (2004). *Teaching online: A practical guide.* Boston, MA: Houghton Mifflin.

Marek, K. (2009). Learning to teach online: Creating a culture of support for faculty. *Journal of Education for Library & Information Science, 50*(4), 275–292.

Moallem, M. (2007). Accommodating individual differences in the design of online learning environments: A comparative study. *Journal of Research on Technology in Education, 40*(2), 217–245.

Norton, P. & Hathaway, D. (2008). Exploring two teacher education online learning designs: A classroom of one or many? *Journal of Research on Technology in Education, 40*(4), 475–495.

Smith, R. (2008). *Conquering the content: A step-by-step guide to online course design.* San Francisco, CA: Jossey-Bass.

Swan, K. (2010). Teaching and learning in post-industrial distance education. In M. F. Cleveland Innes & D. R. Garrison (Eds.), *An introduction to distance education: Understanding teaching and learning in a new era* (pp. 108–134). New York: Routledge.

Wang, L., & Morgan, W. (2008). Student perceptions of using instant messaging software to facilitate synchronous online class interaction in a graduate teacher education course. *Journal of Computing in Teacher Education, 25*(1), 15–21.

CHAPTER 8

VISUALIZE MORE

Effective Online Teaching Methods

Jay Richard Akkerman
Northwest Nazarene University

From grocery stores and airports, to restaurants and the urban intersections of Tokyo, London, Johannesburg, Toronto, New York and beyond, our twenty-first century visual senses are bombarded daily. Today video screens can be found just about everywhere from smart phones, mall checkouts, ATMs, automobile dashboards, and even gas pumps (Akkerman, 2008).

In spite of this, too many educators still fail to visualize their online courses as little more than a vehicle for digital text delivery of their lecture notes, student papers, and threaded discussion board posts. While the sense of sight is necessary for decoding written text, reading alone is a fairly limited use of this important human sense. Thanks to ongoing technological advances being utilized by online learning management providers, educators are learning to appeal more to their students' visual capacities and to expand their learning environments in more graphically expansive ways.

Best Practices of Online Education, pages 91–100
Copyright © 2012 by Information Age Publishing

VISUALIZE

Regardless of age, today's adults are visually attuned across the generational spectrum (Akkerman, 2004), and online educators need to learn new ways of expanding their teaching bandwidth beyond conveying only blocks of text on their students' computer screens. This can be especially challenging for educators whose love of reading has led to a textual bias in their online teaching. Sweet (2001) notes that younger generations have an innate skill set he calls "graphicacy." Moore and Wilson (2006) encourage those who are more textually-attuned to develop this ability, noting that "the key to such transformation is in understanding that the screen is a visual medium, not a textual medium" (p. 20). As mobile, video, and streaming technologies grow more prominent and accessible for online educators, it will no longer be enough for educators to simply *write* the word or *say* the word— we also need to *show* it to our students.

For those in Christian higher education, this conversation should not come as anything new. For many centuries prior to the Enlightenment, followers of Jesus understood the importance of communicating meaning in visual terms (Moore & Wilson, 2006). When Christianity became the official state religion as a result of Constantine's conversion in the fourth century A.D., most of the populace was unable to read. Faced with the pressing need to connect with an empire of Christians who had been converted by statute, the Church was forced to accommodate its teaching methods for those who were accustomed to visual representations as their basis for comprehension. Over the centuries that followed, Christian art and ecclesiastical architecture became vehicles for the indoctrination of preliterate catechumenates through the use of religious sculpture, stained glass, artwork, icons, friezes, doors, and furnishings (Akkerman, 2004; de Borchgrave, 2000; Diebold, 2000).

With the reign of the Holy Roman Empire, the visual arts took their ascendancy in the Church. Rich mosaics and elaborate paintings became more than visual narratives only; instead, they were designed to reinforce the teachings of the faith by complementing the liturgy (Akkerman, 2004; Goethals, 1990). For over a millennium, the Church buttressed its use of Christian imagery on several grounds. Chief among them was the instruction of the illiterate peasant masses. A second use of Christian imagery was to activate the message of Scripture in the memory and imagination. As the Dominican Fra Michele da Carcano observed, "Images were introduced because many people cannot retain in their memories what they hear, but they do remember if they see images" (Baxandall, 1972, p. 41). In recent decades, research by many educational and cognitive psychologists has supported this ancient observation, which has now grown to be called visual learning theory (Palloff & Pratt, 2003). Advocates assert that enhanced learning can occur when instructors convey course information both verbally and visually, noting that "visual literacy accelerates learning because the richness of the whole picture can be taken in at a glance" (Cross, 2011, n.p.).

By the end of the sixth century, aniconic attitudes rose within the Church (Wilson, 1995). As a result, Gregory the Great sanctioned the use of imagery while cautioning against venerating Christian art—an attitude that grew through the Enlightenment and continues to shape much of Western Christendom today. Despite his cautions, Gregory recognized the value of visual representation and insisted that "icons are for the unlettered what the Sacred Scriptures are for the lettered" (Clendenin, 1995, p. 33).

The spoken and written word became more prominent in the Church with the advent of the printing press as ever-increasing numbers of Christians became literate. Yet for educators today, our challenge may not be so much that students are *unable* to read (Akkerman, 2004). Certainly, those of us in higher education hope this is not true of our students! But modern research in literacy studies reveals that literacy and illiteracy are more complex than merely focusing on whether a person can read or not. Yaghjian (1995) relates literacy forms in biblical cultures on a continuum, noting subtle distinctions in terms of a gradation of literacy forms including auraliteracy, oraliteracy, oculiteracy, and scribaliteracy. Schwarz (1981), Jensen (1993) and Akkerman (2004) have explored postliteracy as an additional literacy form at work today. Considering the growing number of people today who seem to prefer to gain information by means other than the printed page, online educators need to consider the impact that visual media can have for learning.

VISUALIZE MORE

When I first began teaching online, the practical training guides available to me focused very little on using visual media in my online courses. This is not surprising since I taught my first online course at a time when many of my students and I were still using 28k modems. Given such limited data transfer capabilities, we were limited largely to text-based course shells in order to deliver content as quickly as possible and in ways that did not overwhelm the digital storage available on our university's servers. Online education was still in its relative infancy, and as an early adopter of the Internet, I was waiting in anticipation for much of what Microsoft co-founder Bill Gates described prophetically at the time:

> It is hard for a teacher to prepare in-depth, interesting material for twenty-five students, six hours a day, 180 days a year. This is particularly true if students' extensive television watching has raised their entertainment expectations. I

can imagine a middle-school science teacher a decade or so from now, working on a lecture about the sun, explaining not only the science but also the history of discoveries that made it possible. When a teacher wants to select a picture, still or video, whether it's a piece of art or a portrait of a great solar scientist, the [Internet super] highway will allow her to select from a comprehensive catalog of images. Snippets of video and narrated animations from countless sources will be available. It will only take minutes to pull together a visual show that would now require days of work to organize. As she lectures about the sun, she will have images and diagrams appear at appropriate times. If a student asks her about the source of the sun's power, she can answer using animated graphics of hydrogen and helium atoms, she'll be able to show solar flares or sunspots or other phenomena, or she might call up a brief video on fusion energy to the white board. The teacher will have organized the links to servers on the information highway in advance. She will make the list of links available to her students, so that during study times in the library or at home, they will be able to review the material from as many perspectives as they find helpful. (Gates 1995, p. 189)

Today's online educators know firsthand that what Bill Gates potentialized in the mid-90s for the classroom can now be realized online. With the proliferation of broadband access today, online faculty and students are now able to utilize visual components much more freely. Fortunately, today's students can now access richer forms of media beyond the bland screens of text that once filled their online course shells. Given this advancement, online faculty members should recognize the opportunity that visual design can have on their instructional design.

The balance of this chapter will explore a few lessons offered by Eliot Noyes, who in 1956 helped Thomas Watson Jr. launch IBM's first corporate design program. After following in his father's footsteps as corporate CEO, Watson Jr. recognized that good design could be a silent partner for Big Blue. In 1973, Watson Jr. remarked in a now famous lecture at the University of Pennsylvania that "good design is good business" (Green, 2011b, n.p.). One should note that IBM's CEO did not merely say, "design is good for business;" Instead, he underscored the importance of *good* design. Good design can be good for learning, too. In the same way that the ancient Church learned to "speak visually" to the illiterate masses, online faculty members in Christian higher education can use good design to engage visually their postliterate students, many of whom now prefer to gain information by means other than the printed page.

Prior to joining IBM, Noyes was an architect and had served previously as the curator of industrial design at MoMA, the Museum of Modern Art in New York City. As a modernist, Noyes believed that "in a sense, a corporation should be like a good painting; everything visible should contribute to the correct total statement; nothing visible should detract. Thus, a company's buildings, offices, graphic design and so forth should all contribute to a total statement about the significance and direction of the company" (Green, 2011d, n.p.). Watson Jr. supported this vision enthusiastically and personalized Noyes's corporate metaphor. When asked for IBM's definition of good design, Watson Jr. answered, "We feel that good design must primarily serve people, and not the other way around" (Green, 2011c, n.p.). The IBM Selectric is a good case in point; Noyes was responsible for the streamlined form and sculptural beauty of this innovation that transformed the electric business typewriter so much that this IBM classic was found on the office desks of most secretaries in corporate America for more than a generation (Brill, 2011).

As online educators, we must always recognize that visual content in our course shells serves our students and the learning process, not vice-versa. Visual content can take many forms, including font color and selection, proportional white space on the screen, the use of graphical links in place of textual ones, graphic headers for course shells, and the use of slideshows, images, and streaming video, to name a few. In considering visual design, Noyes boiled down his personalized principles to four simple steps. He affirmed that good design: first, fulfills its function; second, respects its materials; third, is suited to the method of production; and fourth, combines these in imaginative expressions (Green, 2011d). Noyes's list can also apply to online course design, and the balance of this chapter will explore the implications of these four principles for online educators.

When designing online courses, faculty members must recognize two important things: first, that form can often take precedence over function; and second, that visual elements are not merely decorative. As a longtime consultant to Noyes, Charles Eames noted that good design is a plan for arranging elements in ways that best accomplish their defined purpose. Richard Sapper, who was a colleague of Eames, noted in a 1992 article in IBM's iconic corporate magazine titled *Think* that "Any product with the IBM logo is an ambassador of the corporation. And each product's design is an integral element of its quality. It's not simply a matter of aesthetics; design reflects and enhances the company's reputation and prestige" (Green, 2011a, n.p.).

Mundane visual form can inhibit educational function. Online course shells filled only with screens full of text are the digital counterparts to traditional classrooms devoid of any visual learning tools. For visually attuned students, these online courses are poor visual ambassadors for their educational institutions. Instead, online faculty are encouraged to create a design standard for their courses, utilizing good design principles that reflect the professor's own uniqueness and that connect the symbolic with the more rational aspects of their courses. Depending on its purpose, visual content in online courses can function in a variety of ways. For instance, Moore & Wilson (2006) note that "Each font that a designer chooses to put on the screen (or in print) speaks with a voice that should compliment [sic] the theme. Many fonts evoke feelings, and those feelings can eclipse the syntactical meaning of the text" (p. 78). At the most basic level, online courses built around a clean graphic design convey organization, invite interest, and minimize student fatigue. Font selection and adequate negative space are two fundamental ways to strengthen the visual impact for an online course.

In the same way that *USA Today* works strategically from a limited palette of fonts, professors should learn to develop and utilize a consistent font scheme throughout their course shells so they can be read easily and underscore their design standard. While conventional wisdom has held that fonts with serifs, the semi-structural elements on the ends of many letter strokes, are easier to read than their sans serif counterparts, researchers have not yet formed "a concrete body of theoretical knowledge on the part that serifs may play in legibility" (Poole, 2011, n.p.). After extensive review of the research, Poole (2011) admits simply that "we should accept that most reasonably designed typefaces in mainstream use will be equally legible" (n.p.). When considering a typeface for use in course shells, choose a font that is among those that are common to both Windows and Mac users. Choosing from font families that are available universally to all students enables consistent display by everyone in the class. In most cases, this will likely be a sans serif font like Arial, Lucida, Tahoma, Trebuchet, or Verdana, or a serif font like Georgia, Palatino Linotype, or Times New Roman. Online professors may want to consider using both display and body fonts consistently throughout a course. Display fonts can be understood as "headline fonts" that are often larger, bolder, and are used to draw attention, while body fonts are smaller and are read more easily in large blocks. Regardless of whether one chooses a single font or utilizes both display and body fonts, online course designers should recognize that a font scheme should be utilized beyond the course shell itself; whenever possible, the same font style should also be displayed consistently in one's syllabus, course documents, slide shows, and videos to underscore that course's design standard.

Learning management systems like ANGEL or Blackboard are designed to format page layout in ways that incorporate adequate negative space on the screen. Whether on screen or on the printed page, negative space is the portion that is blank or devoid of text or graphics. Margins and the space between lines of text also contribute to negative space, which rests the eye and conveys a cleaner look to the page. Again, the need for adequate amounts of negative space needs to be extended to other visual course elements as noted above. Given that a great deal of online learning is conveyed in text form, it is important to recognize that the space itself around text and graphics is in fact a visual representation that can reduce viewer fatigue, thereby strengthening student learning.

Noyes underscored the importance of good design respecting its materials. In online learning, our materials are not primarily physical, but digital.

For both students and faculty, issues like access speed and memory allocations on both the user's computer and also the server/s become essential in utilizing online course content. Unfortunately, video and audio course elements require much more memory and take longer to access than their textually-based counterparts. Yet ongoing improvements to these technologies seem to change at an ever-expanding rate, making them more accessible in online education than ever before. In online courses, audio and video content can be optimized in ways that reduce the amount of memory required, especially when this is paired with shorter-length lecture recordings. Given that one's screen resolution or the maximum density of video pixels per square inch (dpi) is limited in most cases to 72, one should not create graphics for online display at any higher resolution. To illustrate: on a 72 dpi monitor, a 300 dpi graphic will display only at 72 dpi. Therefore, saving graphics files at higher resolutions is a waste of server space. Online faculty members are also encouraged to use streaming media and podcast technologies for easier and secured student access. In many cases, it is optimal to link such content from an external server or content repository to one's course shell.

According to Noyes, good design is also suited to the method of production. In an online environment, course designers must consider how one's visual design can be developed, especially when designers believe they "don't have a creative bone in their bodies." One fairly straightforward way to strengthen visually an online course is through the use of a graphic header. Fortunately, powerful but straightforward graphics packages like Adobe Photoshop/Elements are relatively inexpensive to both Apple and Windows users and empower them to create a professional-looking header that can be used consistently on all course syllabi, assignment templates, written lectures, transcripts, and the like. Photoshop/Elements is significantly less expensive than its full-blown professional counterpart and can be mastered easily to produce good quality layered graphics that can be saved and displayed with a resolution of 72 dpi for online viewing. Similarly, the use of photos, graphs, and tables can be helpful in conveying information in visual terms, whether they are in a course syllabus or a digitized lecture manuscript.

Noyes's final step calls for the combination of design cues in what he calls "imaginative expression" (Green, 2011d). Today, online course designers are encouraged to "tune their eyes" toward the growing number of ways information is expressed visually. Advertisers are masters at saying a great deal with few, if any, words. Consider the ways that leading information providers convey their content online and in print, regardless of whether they are news magazines, television advertisers, entertainers, or blog sites. As an educator, commit yourself to learning from such sources. Your students will likely thank you one day.

Of course, online educators who desire to improve the visual experience of students in their courses need to be cautious about going overboard and actually hindering the learning experience with too much visual stimulation. Bartoletti (2011) cautions that the "improper use of fonts, colors, and graphics can also serve as a distraction and hamper the effectiveness of your course" (n.p.). Maintaining appropriate balances among text, image, and sound is key. "More" is a relative term that calls for assessment by faculty, students, and those who review an institution's online courses on an ongoing basis. By the same token, faculty members who do not see themselves as particularly creative people need not be intimidated. By utilizing a few straightforward design principles, even professors who don't consider themselves artistic at all can create online courses that are more visually engaging.

A final note: online faculty members are wise to be reminded that their students have much to teach them, too. Faculty with dominant textual preferences can learn from more visually-attuned students by seeing how they complete assignments that exercise the more creative, right hemisphere of their brains (Edwards, 1999). Additionally, even those who teach in asynchronous online environments can learn to connect from time to time with their students via live web conferencing applications like Adobe Connect or Skype. In such cases, faculty members can make themselves available to their students in real time through virtual office hours or by connecting via a live webcam with students at a predetermined time. Even though my online courses are designed to be asynchronous, I have found in recent years that nearly all of my students are eager to chat with me live during my courses. The use of these technologies not only permits live voice conversations, but it also adds video to the spectrum for one or both of us for little or no cost to either party. Some applications like Adobe Connect also permit the facilitator to save the webcast in streaming format for later student use, while new web-based graphical technologies like Second Life are already opening new doors to what virtual interaction is beginning to look like (Lu, 2010).

As with any new life lesson, we first often have to face bad habits that must be changed. Many online educators need to think differently about their teaching—this time with a more visual group of students in mind. There is nothing magical about using visual media in teaching; students are not controlled remotely by its use. By the same token, expanding online course content beyond purely text-based delivery can be helpful to both professors and students alike. In such cases, this kind of faculty-student interaction can be more engaging, especially for those who are more visually-attuned.

DISCUSSION QUESTIONS

1. Describe your innate learning preference: do you tend to be more of a textually based learner or a more visually-attuned one? How does this relate to your teaching style? What benefits come naturally to your preferred style? What are some of the inherent weaknesses of your style? How might you overcome these?

2. If you are teaching online already, open one of your course shells. If you wear glasses, take them off. If not, blur your vision. What do you see? Are your page views vast seas of grey text lines? How might you begin to make your course shells more "visible"?

3. Look at your course assignments. Are they geared exclusively to written projects? Consider student assignments that also require more creative visual input. For instance, invite students to develop their own proposals for creative projects that could be done in conjunction with a written assignment. Let your students help you better understand how visual projects can communicate their newfound discoveries.

4. Even if your course is asynchronous, strongly encourage your students to connect with you at least one time via online teleconferencing, either individually or in smaller clusters. Use resources like Adobe Connect or Skype to conduct these live, more personal conferences with your students. You'll be amazed by the impact that seeing and hearing one another can have on rapport and understanding.

5. Introduce some basic visual elements in your course shell by inserting graphic links in place of textual hyperlinks. Basic software like Adobe Photoshop/Elements can empower faculty members to create attractive bars that can be inserted into most course management systems. For instance, create an attractive bar that reads, "Click here for streaming media." After creating the graphic, insert it into your content area, then highlight the graphic and imbed your hyperlink in it. Then, students can simply click on the graphic bar to go to their desired destination.

6. Explore virtual social communities by creating a free account in Second Life (www.secondlife.com). What kind of opportunities could exist for online education in a virtual environment like this? What kind of cautions would you need to consider?

REFERENCES

Akkerman, J. R. (2004). *The graphic gospel: Preaching in a postliterate age* (Doctoral dissertation). Asbury Theological Seminary, Wilmore, KY. Retrieved from Dissertation Abstracts International. (UMI No. TX6042601)

Akkerman, J. R. (2008). Remote control or remote chaos? *Holiness Today*, September/October 2008, 18–19.

Bartoletti, R. (2011, July 11). Visual design for distance education content. Retrieved from http://cnx.org/content/m17297/latest/?collection=col10556/latest

Baxandall, M. (1972). *Painting and experience in fifteenth century Italy*. New York: Oxford.

Brill, E. (2011). The Selectric typewriter: Overview. Retrieved June 19, 2011, from http://www.ibm.com/ibm100/us/en/icons/selectric/

Clendenin, D. B. (1995). From the verbal to the visual: Orthodox icons and the sanctification of sight. *Christian Scholars Review, 25*(3), 30–46.

Cross, J. (2011). Why use visuals? Seeing the meaning: Exploring visual learning on MirandaNet. Retrieved June 10, 2011, from http://www.mirandanet.ac.uk/vl_blog/?page_id=122

de Borchgrave, H. (2000). *A journey into Christian art*. Minneapolis, MI: Fortress.

Diebold, W. J. (2000). *Word and image: An introduction to early medieval art*. Boulder, CO: Westview.

Edwards, B. (1999). *The new drawing on the right side of the brain*. New York: Penguin.

Gates, B. (1995) *The road ahead*. New York: Viking.

Goethals, G. T. (1990). *The electronic golden calf: Images, religion, and the making of meaning*. Cambridge, MA: Cowley.

Green, L. (2011a). Good design is good business: In their words. Retrieved May 15, 2011, from http://www.ibm.com/ibm100/us/en/icons/gooddesign/words/

Green, L. (2011b). Good design is good business: Overview. Retrieved May 15, 2011, from http://www.ibm.com/ibm100/us/en/icons/gooddesign/

Green, L. (2011c). Good design is good business: The team. Retrieved May 15, 2011, from http://www.ibm.com/ibm100/us/en/icons/gooddesign/team/

Green, L. (2011d). Lee. Good design is good business: Transforming the world. Retrieved May 15, 2011, from http://www.ibm.com/ibm100/us/en/icons/gooddesign/transform/

Jensen, R. A. (1993). *Thinking in story: Preaching in a post-literate age*. Lima, OH: C. S. S

Lu, L. (2010). Art café @ second life. *Art Education, 63*. Retrieved from EBSCOhost.

Moore, J., & Wilson, L. (2006). *Design matters: Creating powerful imagery for worship*. Nashville, TN: Abingdon.

Palloff, R. M. & Pratt, K. (2003). *The virtual student*. Hoboken, NJ: Jossey-Bass.

Poole, A. (2011). Which are more legible: Serif or sans serif typefaces? Retrieved June 30, 2011, from http://alexpoole.info/which-are-more-legible-serif-or-sans-serif-typefaces

Schwarz, T. (1981). *The second god*. New York: Random House.

Sweet, L. (2001). *Carpe manana*. Grand Rapids, MI: Zondervan.

Wilson, L. (1995). *Redefining literacy: The church in an electronic age* (Unpublished master's thesis). United Theological Seminary, Dayton, OH.

Yaghjian, L. (1995). Ancient reading. In R. L. Rohrbaugh (Ed.), *The sciences and New Testament interpretation* (pp. 206–230). Peabody, MA: Hendrickson.

CHAPTER 9

CHARACTERISTICS OF SUCCESSFUL ONLINE STUDENTS

Jason D. Baker
Regent University

What makes a successful online learner? This is a significant question for institutions and prospective students alike. Unlike some higher education institutions, Christian colleges and seminaries typically eschew the "look to your left and right, one of these students will drop out" mentality. Rather, in seeking to promote the integration of faith and learning and supporting students as fellow image-bearers of God, Christian schools seek to create effective and supportive learning environments instead of competitive ones. Similarly, prospective students (or their parents or employers) are investing a significant amount of time and money into pursuit of a degree and want to ensure that they get a reasonable return on their investment. At the very least, they want to graduate.

There are some characteristics about the online environment that should be considered to determine whether someone would make a successful online learner. This chapter gives clarity to some myths of online learning and provides characteristics of successful online learners.

Best Practices of Online Education, pages 101–106
Copyright © 2012 by Information Age Publishing
All rights of reproduction in any form reserved.

MYTHS OF THE ONLINE CLASSROOM

There used to be a commercial that ran on our local radio station that promoted an online MBA program. The announcer asked if you were juggling work, family, and other activities and wanted to earn an MBA but could not because your schedule was too full to attend classes on campus. If this described you, the announcer said that online learning was the solution because you could earn your degree while juggling everything else at the same time. While this doesn't come right out and claim that online learning is less work than traditional courses, the implication is that you can fit online learning around a hyper-busy life and succeed. Online learning takes time, often more time than the traditional classroom since structured class sessions are replaced by multiple learning activities. Additionally, it often takes longer to write something to contribute to an online discussion than to say the same words orally in a face-to-face discussion. The idea that online learning does not require a significant investment in time is a myth. Online courses take at least as much time as their campus counterparts and sometimes significantly more time. If you enter an online learning program with any other expectation, you are likely to be frustrated, and this can result in dropping the course.

Another myth of online classes is that they function like independent studies. In other words, I can cram an entire semester into a couple of weekends and then earn the course grade or at least coast for the remainder of the term. This myth does not say that online learning is easy but that learners have complete control over scheduling their learning activities and can fit them in whenever they wish. While some online courses are structured this way, many follow a traditional semester schedule. Often students are required to participate in weekly activities throughout the semester and are simply unable to fit an entire class into their personal schedules. It is important to look carefully at the way courses and degree programs are structured before committing to one.

The final myth is that all online courses are alike. Someone takes an online class, perhaps designed as an asynchronous, seminar-style, discussion-rich course, and he or she assumes that all online classes are that way. Such an expectation is shattered when the same student enrolls in a course that depends more on synchronous web-conferencing classes with a large number of individual papers and projects and very little use of threaded discussion boards. Growing up in traditional schools, many of us recognize that there is a wide variety in classroom styles, from large lecture halls to small class seminars, from hands-on labs to textbook-laden exams. Just as there is no one size fits all traditional course, there is no single model of online courses. Some are large, others are small; some meet synchronously while others are entirely asynchronous; some use rich media and social networking and others rely on presentations and lecture notes. It is important to recognize this diversity, as various design approaches work better for different students. Some may perform well in one model and poorly in another. This is why you should align your learning preferences with a suitable online design model to increase your likelihood of success.

SUCCEEDING AS AN ONLINE LEARNER

Despite the diversity of online instructional models, the commonality of the online environment means that there are a number of characteristics and skills that successful online learners share. These include technological resources and literacy, strong reading skills, the ability to communicate effectively via writing, good time management, willingness to seek help when in need, and a degree of independence and learner autonomy. While it's certainly possible to succeed online without all of these attributes, having them will make the online learning experience richer and probably more enjoyable as well.

Technological literacy is an obvious skill for a successful online learner. You do not have to be a computer science major, but if you are not fluent in email, web browsing, and office applications, then perhaps this is not the best choice. In addition to literacy, you also want to have a quality computer system with a fast and stable Internet connection. Although there was a time when you could successfully navigate online courses via an old computer and dial-up connection, contemporary learning management systems and increasing use of rich media (e.g., audio, video, web conferencing, etc.) demand a current system with a broadband connection.

While reading skills may not be the first thing that comes to mind when you think of online learning, they are essential to success. Whereas many face-to-face classes are built on lectures, the best practices in online course design stress that simply streaming lectures is not effective and that you need to engage students through a variety of other means. As a result, lectures have often been replaced by instructor notes, texts, and supplementary reading materials in addition to audio podcasts, video presentations, and other rich media resources. In other words, while many traditional classes combined instructor lecturing with outside reading, many online courses replace the former with the latter, thus resulting in an increased amount of reading material for an online course. Therefore, it is critical that you are not only a good reader but have the ability to retain information learned from reading, so examine your options carefully if you are someone who is much more attuned to audio-based learning.

Just as the amount of reading has increased in many online classes, so has the amount of writing. In addition to writing papers and other written materials for assignments, often the actual in-class communication is conducted via online discussions. Most frequently these are asynchronous threaded discussion boards where instructors will post questions and then the students (and instructor) will engage in a spirited dialogue about the topics under consideration. This is analogous to an in-class discussion in a traditional course except in this case the entire discussion is written down and posted online. Therefore, you need to be comfortable not only writing papers but doing the bulk of your communication in writing. This includes asking questions of the instructor, collaborating with peers, and even praying for one another. I suspect that the growth of Facebook has increased many people's comfort levels with using online writing for personal communication. However, I will confess that it feels unusual at first to write down prayers—although we find them written throughout the Bible—but that's a regular occurrence in Christian online learning. If you want to succeed online, make sure that you are comfortable reading and writing interpersonal, logistical, and content-oriented interaction.

Time management is also an essential skill to master if you are going to succeed online. Not surprisingly, effective time management is important for any learning endeavor, but the mediated nature of the online environment makes this a particularly critical skill. Traditional classes meet one or more times a week on campus, which serves as a helpful rhythm to keep students on track. Besides, showing up to class unprepared can cause a great deal of embarrassment, particularly if the professor calls on you. In the online environment you typically have neither the regularly scheduled meetings nor the pressure of being called on in a live session. Therefore, what is intended to be a flexible anytime, anyplace learning opportunity can devolve into a no time, no place experience for someone who does not manage his or her time well. Additionally, if you're not logging in regularly to the online course environment, you can become overwhelmed with all of the posts and materials to read when you do finally log in. Speaking from personal experience, logging into a discussion board and finding hundreds of unread posts is enough to make you want to give up. Therefore, it is important that you plan your course out carefully and schedule your time.

Be sure to communicate to family, employers, friends, and others that you are enrolled in an online course and that you need to block off time to devote to your learning. Traditional students are used to weekly class time on campus plus additional homework time for reading and assignments. However, in the online course, your so-called homework time includes the equivalent of the campus class time. Therefore you need to block off large quantities of time for online learning. Sometimes you use this time to catch up on email or discussion board posts, other times will be spent reading books or online materials, and still other times will be devoted to completing your course assignments. Consider not only scheduling time but also setting aside a dedicated place to complete your courses. Working on a laptop at your kitchen table can be difficult because your materials are shoved aside at dinnertime. Whether at a library, a home office, or even an end table, it is easier to focus on your studies if you have a place to go where you (and others) know it is reserved for learning.

If you have ever been in a really large lecture course, you know the experience of being a student number with minimal contact with the instructor. In such cases, you often ask other students for clarification when you are confused or lost. In the online learning world, however, it is important that you become comfortable raising your virtual hand and asking for help from your instructor when necessary. It can be uncomfortable for many who fear that they look foolish asking a question or who are used to deferring to authority figures and have never questioned professors. In the virtual classroom, however, professors do not know if students are confused unless they let the instructor know. Unless there is a two-way videoconference associated with the online course, faculty cannot read the nonverbal cues of students. Therefore, please do not hesitate to ask questions of your instructor. You are not being disrespectful, you are being helpful and others in your class are likely harboring the same question.

Finally, even though many online courses are designed to promote collaboration and community, it helps to have a high degree of independence and learner autonomy. Despite the many successful efforts to promote learning communities online, there is a level of self-motivation that online students report that they need to a greater extent than in their traditional learning experiences. This does not mean that you are isolated, but without the experiences of sitting in the same classroom with other students, having impromptu conversations after class, forming study groups at the local coffeehouse, or just seeing your professor in person, it is easy for some students to become discouraged. Be a self-starter and do not wait for the professor or others to pull you along. You need to take charge of your own learning and be an active participant in the process.

CONCLUSION

Contrary to some perceptions, online learning may be more difficult than traditional classes. Some students have a difficult time with the increased level of self-discipline and personal responsibility associated with online learning. Others may actually work better in the online environment because it fits their personality. For example, introverted learners may find online class discussions easier to participate in than face-to-face discussions since they have time to formulate a response before posting. So while online learning might involve significantly more work, the flexibility might make it a better fit for some students.

Online learning is not for everyone. Ask yourself the following questions: Am I comfortable using the Internet? Do I have a fast and stable Internet connection? Am I a strong reader? Am I a strong writer? Can I communicate well with others via email? Do I manage my time well? Can I get tasks done without having someone personally remind me? Can I reserve time for studying even if I do not have regular class meeting times? If the answers to most of these questions are yes, then online learning might work well for you. If not, then perhaps you would be better off taking a traditional course.

Finally, as Christian students, please always remember to treat one another with grace and love. One of the challenges of online learning is that all communication is mediated, via email, discussion boards, podcasts, videoconferences, or other forms of technology. When we are behind the safety of a computer screen, it is easy to lose site of the other end of the interaction, where another person is sitting at his or her computer screen. Like you, that person is also made in the image of God and warrants treatment accordingly. Many difficulties in the online learning experience could be resolved quickly and effectively if participants remembered Paul's admonition in I Corinthians 13 that knowledge will pass away but love will remain.

DISCUSSION QUESTIONS

1. Does online learning work well for everyone?
2. Which of these characteristics of successful online learners is most important?
3. Which characteristic is your strongest? How might you help others with your strength?
4. Which characteristic is your weakest? How might you work to improve in this area?
5. What type of online class would be best suited to your personality and abilities?

RECOMMENDED READING

Bowman, L. (2010). *Online learning: A user-friendly approach for high school and college students.* Lanham, MD: Rowman & Littlefield.

Brosche, T. A. M. & Feavel, M. (Eds.). (2011). *Successful online learning: Managing the online learning environment efficiently and effectively.* Sudbury, MA: Jones & Bartlett.

White, K. W. & Baker, J. D. (Eds.). (2004). *The student guide to successful online learning: A handbook of tips, strategies, and techniques.* Needham Heights, MA: Allyn & Bacon.

CHAPTER 10

GENERATING AND FACILITATING EFFECTIVE ONLINE DISCUSSION

Mark A. Maddix
Northwest Nazarene University

INTRODUCTION

Online interaction has always been a key component of an online course. Whether it is student-to-student or student-to-teacher interaction, the ability to discuss and exchange ideas has long been considered the component that adds value to an online course. This is what distinguishes online courses from correspondence courses, where written materials are posted on a webpage for students to access. Most online courses and programs promote the highly interactive nature of their curriculum as evidence of their educational philosophy (Lorenzetti, 2010). The success of effective online courses is dependent on the quality of interaction in online discussion forums. Online teachers agree that online discussions forums are the most important avenue for learning to happen. The power of discussion forums is that teachers and students can thoughtfully add to a discussion based on their own time schedule. This is not often possible in a traditional classroom where all students may not have the opportunity to contribute.

Best Practices of Online Education, pages 107–119

Effective online discussions can create a dynamic learning context that fosters learning, growth, and community among students and the teacher.

However, the challenge for teachers is to ensure that discussion fosters effective learning and formation. This is especially true when online courses include three times the student interaction than a traditional face-to-face course. For teachers facilitating discussion it can become an overwhelming task, especially when there is too much or not enough student interaction. The complexity of generating and facilitating effective online discussion is critical to the success of an online class. Teachers are challenged to address such questions as: How do you ensure that discussion is contributing to learning? How much interaction is necessary and what constitutes effective interaction? How can I ensure that students engage in thoughtful discussion? These perplexing questions and others are addressed in this chapter. This chapter also presents the Community Inquiry Model as a framework for effective online discussion (Garrison & Anderson, 2011). This chapter explores how to develop online discussion board rubrics, and how to ensure faculty and student interaction in online courses. It concludes by providing best practices of online discussion based on current research and personal experience in teaching online courses.

SYNCHRONOUS OR ASYNCHRONOUS DISCUSSION

In distant learning contexts there are two types of online discussion. One is synchronous, which includes real time discussions, and the other is asynchronous, which includes online discussions that do not take place in real time. In most online courses asynchronous online discussions have become most widely used to support student interaction. An asynchronous online discussion is a text-based computer-mediated communication that allows human-to-human interaction without time and location constraints (Xie, Durrington, & Yen, 2011). Research suggests that asynchronous online discussions have many positive attributes in online learning. Online discussions enable convenient interactions between student and students and students and teachers. The facilitation of online discussion extends collaborative knowledge construction and information distribution as well as supporting cognitive and metacognitive engagement of reasoning and argumentation (Xie, Vance, & Ling, 2011). The successes of online discussions have been connected to the attitude of students particularly in fostering a sense of community and relationships.

Since the majority of online courses include asynchronous online discussion forums, the primary focus of this chapter is to discover how to develop effective asynchronous discussions. Also, research indicates that the most effective asynchronous courses include some synchronous online discussions. For example some online courses use Skye, Jing, or Adobe Connect to provide real time video discussions. The benefits of providing these synchronous online discussions are in building relationships between students and faculty and providing an opportunity for live interaction. It is recommended that online classes include both asynchronous and synchronous online discussions.

COMMUNITY OF INQUIRY MODEL (CIM)

The Community of Inquiry Model (CIM) was developed by D. R. Garrison and Terry Anderson (2003) to achieve a high level of student learning in online discussion. According to Garrison and Anderson (2003), "A critical community of learners, from an educational perspective, is composed of teachers and students transacting with the specific purposes of facilitating, constructing, and validating understanding, and of developing capabilities that will lead to further learning. Such a community encourages cognitive independence and social interdependence simultaneously" (p. 23). A CIM is a group of individuals who collaboratively engage in purposeful critical discourse and reflection to construct meaning and confirm mutual understanding. The CIM theoretical framework represents a process of creating a deep and meaningful collaborative and constructivist learning experience through the development of three interdependent elements: (a) cognitive presence, (b) social presence, and (c) teaching presence (See Figure 10.1). These interdependent elements provide a framework to measure and evaluate learning outcomes in online discussion forums. Based on the CIM, online discussion can be generated and facilitated for effective learning and formation.

Here is a brief description of each of the three interdependent elements:

Cognitive Presence is the extent to which the participants in any particular configuration of a community of inquiry are able to construct meaning through sustained communication. In essence, cognitive presence is a condition of higher order thinking and learning. The primary focus on cognitive presence is to ensure that online discussion and dialogue includes learning exercises that foster critical thinking.

Social Presence is the ability of learners to project their personal characteristics into the community of inquiry by presenting themselves as "real people." Due to the lack of non-verbal communication, the shift from spoken communication to written communication presents a challenge for establishing social presence (Garrison & Anderson, 2003). The frequency of written communication and presence of faculty interaction enhances cognitive presence. In other words, the frequency of student and faculty interaction enhances the student's ability to engage in higher levels of criti-

Community of Inquiry

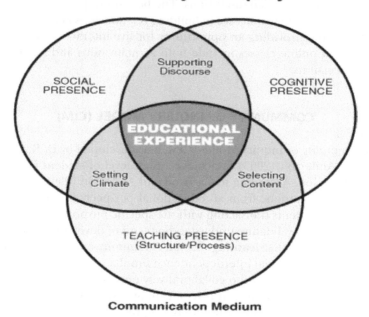

Figure 10.1 Community of Inquiry model (Garrison and Anderson, 2003, p. 29).

cal thinking. The function of this element is to support the cognitive and affective objectives of learning. Social presence supports cognitive objectives through its ability to instigate, sustain, and support critical thinking in online discussion forums (Rourke, Anderson, Garrison, & Archer, 2001).

Teaching Presence is defined as the design, facilitation, and direction of cognitive and social processes for the purpose of realizing personally meaningful and educationally worthwhile learning outcomes (Garrison & Anderson, 2003). The teacher brings all the aspects of the learning process together to meet the learning outcomes and the respective needs of the learner. The role of the teacher is critical in generating and facilitating online discussion by structuring appropriate online discussion guidelines to ensure student engagement and learning. This is often the most difficult task in developing an online course, but with intentional course mapping based on the course learning outcomes (see Chapter 12), the teacher can ensure quality in online discussions forums. In the Community of Inquiry Model, teacher and students participate in a learning transaction that is more readily identified with constructivist rather than instructivist approaches to education. Therefore, social presence is regarded as a function of both the teacher and the students.

The Community of Inquiry Model provides a theoretical framework to evaluate effective online discussion through three elements of communication: social, cognitive, and teaching presence. This framework is beneficial to the Christian educator because it provide a holistic approach to learning. It also provides the Christian educator with tools to assess and evaluate effective online discussion.

SEVEN PRINCIPLES OF GOOD PRACTICE

Much of the research about good practices centers on Arthur Chickering and Zelda Gamson's *Seven Principles of good practice in Undergraduate Education* (1991), which was adapted for online education by Arthur Chickering and Stephen Ehrmann in *Implementing the Seven principles: Technology as a Lever* (1996). Even though the seven practices are designed for undergraduate education, they are applicable to all forms of post-secondary education. These seven principles provide a theoretical framework to evaluate effective online learning:

1. *Encourages contact between students and faculty.* Frequent student-faculty contact in and out of classes is the most important factor in student motivation and involvement. Faculty concern helps students get through rough times and keep on working. Knowing a few faculty members well enhances students' intellectual commitment and encourages them to think about their own values and future plans.

2. *Develops reciprocity and cooperation among students.* Learning is enhanced when it is more like a team effort than a solo race. Good learning, like good work, is collaborative and social, not competitive and isolated. Working with others often increases involvement in learning. Sharing one's own ideas and responding to others' reactions sharpens thinking and deepens understanding.

3. *Encourages active learning: Learning is not a spectator sport.* Students do not learn much just by sitting in classes listening to teachers, memorizing pre-packaged assignments, and spitting out answers. They must talk about what they are learning, write about it, relate it to past experiences and apply it to their daily lives. They must make what they learn part of themselves.

4. *Gives prompt feedback: Knowing what you know and don't know focuses learning.* Students need appropriate feedback on performance to benefit from courses. When getting started, students need help in assessing existing knowledge and competence. In classes, students need frequent opportunities to perform and receive suggestions for improvement. At various points during college, and at the end, stu-

dents need chances to reflect on what they have learned, what they still need to know, and how to assess themselves.

5. *Emphasizes time on task: Time plus energy equals learning.* There is no substitute for time on task. Learning to use one's time well is critical for students and professionals alike. Students need help in learning effective time management. Allocating realistic amounts of time means effective learning for students and effective teaching for faculty. How an institution defines time expectations for students, faculty, administrators, and other professional staff can establish the basis of high performance for all.

6. *Communicates high expectations: Expect more and you will get more.* High expectations are important for everyone—for the poorly prepared, for those unwilling to exert themselves, and for the bright and well-motivated. Expecting students to perform well becomes a self-fulfilling prophecy when teachers and institutions hold high expectations for them and make extra efforts.

7. *Respects diverse talents and ways of learning.* There are many roads to learning. People bring different talents and styles of learning to college. Brilliant students in the seminar room may be all thumbs in the lab or art studio. Students rich in hands-on experience may not do so well with theory. Students need the opportunity to show their talents and learn in ways that work for them. Then they can be pushed to learn in new ways that do not come so easily (Chickering & Gamon, 1991).

BEST PRACTICES OF ONLINE EDUCATION

Since online discussion has the benefit of a long history in distant learning courses, there is a wealth of information available to inform best practices of online discussion. The following list is not inclusive of all practices but provides a summary of the best practices from the literature and personal experience in generating and facilitating online discussion.

1. *Develop clear guidelines and expectations for discussion.* The course syllabus should provide clear guidelines and expectations for student and faculty interaction in the discussion board. This should include the number of days of participating in the class in a given week, the number of posts to be submitted each week, the expected time of study during the week, and a clear discussion rubric to evaluate online discussion. Also, the guidelines should include clear expectations about the number of words in a given post (example: 250–500 words) and the frequency of responses (example: four to six peer

responses per week). The teacher also is to clarify his or her availability and response time to student interaction. In most online courses teachers are asked to respond to student interaction within a 24 hour period of time. When developing the course guidelines, provide at least 20 to 30 percent of the course grade to include student-to-student and teacher-to-student interaction. Some advocate that the course should include up to 40 percent of the course grade in interaction, but no less than 10 percent.

2. *Develop discussion rubrics that evaluate cognitive, social, and teaching presence.* Based on the Community of Inquiry Model, the online discussion rubric provides the teacher and student with an objective framework to measure interaction. The rubric can be developed on a five point likert scale to provide objective criteria to measure student interaction (see Appendix 10.1). The teacher is to give student evaluations on a regular basis based on the definition of a substantive post. A substantive post is to include: knowledge (cognitive), grammar/spelling (communication), and timeliness (due date). This is to be reflected in the discussion board rubric. This ensures that quality interaction is taking place in the online course. Also, include discussion etiquette in the course syllabus, which consists of the following:
   - Be sensitive and reflective to what others are saying.
   - Do not use all caps. It is the equivalent of screaming.
   - Do not flame, which are outbursts of extreme emotion or opinion.
   - Think before you hit the post (enter/reply) button. You cannot take it back!
   - Do not use offensive language.
   - Use clear subject lines.
   - Do not use abbreviations or acronyms unless the entire class knows them.
   - Keep the dialog collegial and professional.

   Since online discussion is the heart of online courses it is imperative that the teacher provides clear expectations about how student interaction is to be measured. A robust discussion board rubric is essential to effective online learning.

3. *The teacher is to facilitate and manage online interaction on a regular basis.* The teacher is to facilitate the pace of the course by monitoring the class on a daily basis. This includes answering all outstanding questions for each module or section, providing "whole class" feedback at regular intervals, and being proactive in contacting students who are falling behind in the class discussion (Berge, 1995). Teachers when facilitating online discussion are to avoid two extremes, mothering and orphaning. Mothering is responding too early to student interaction,

which preempts student discussion. Orphaning is allowing the discussion to dissolve into little more than opinions because of insufficient involvement. For the discussion to be educational, it must go beyond uninformed opinions based on unstudied prejudices. The teacher is to assure that students give the evidence supporting their views and refuse to tolerate weak arguments, *ad hominem* attacks, unsupported or undocumented claims, and unclear writing and grammar. If the students do not adequately respond to discussion questions early in the course, the moderator must give some exemplary responses to illustrate how they ought to have done. Thus, the teacher's involvement will usually be more intense early in the course than as the course progresses. Also, the teacher does not have to worry about answering and responding to all student post and responses. The teacher is to read all posts and give specific responses to individual students and more general responses to the class as a whole.

4. *Students should be responsible and committed to the process of online discussion.* Palloff and Pratt (2003) provide the following list of responsibilities in an online learning community. These responsibilities are essential to ensure effective online discussion. They include:
   - *Openness and willingness* to share personal information about work and life outside of school.
   - *Flexibility* by developing an understanding of the nature of online learning and the willingness to "go with the flow."
   - *Honesty* in the willingness to give feedback and share thoughts and concerns in the online discussion forum.
   - *Willingness to take responsibility for community formation* by taking charge of discussion and learning activities. This includes being actively engaged in online discussion on a regular basis.
   - *Willingness to work collaboratively* by demonstrating the ability to work with peers in discussion as well as in collaborative small group activities (Palloff & Pratt 2003).

   Students' participation and engagement in student-to-student and teacher-to-student interaction is dependent on their ability to manage and navigate the course requirements. If students are not active in the online discussion, then it will inhibit individual and communal learning and growth.

5. *Generate discussion by asking good questions.* The instructional design of the course is to include discussion questions that facilitate student dialogue and engagement. Discussion should include open ended questions that encourage critical and creative thinking. Also, discussion questions are to be written to achieve social interaction and community building. In facilitating discussion the teacher is to provide prompt responses to student posts and trigger the discus-

sion by asking questions. At the end of each discussion the teacher can provide a summary of postings to bring the module or topic to a close. When asking students to respond to specific course content and materials, it is appropriate to ask closed ended questions to ensure students comprehend the course materials. There are a variety of ways to further interaction through discussion. Here are some practical examples:

- Ask open-ended questions.
- Ask questions that focus on higher levels of cognition (B. Bloom's Taxonomy).
- Ask probing questions by using the Socratic method.
- When appropriate play the devil's advocate to challenge students' claims.
- Promote divergent and convergent forms of thinking.
- Have students defend their stand or opinions with supporting evidence.
- When possible ask students to relate course content to personal experience.

6. *Create forums for informal and relational connections with students.* In order to develop social presence in the class, the teacher is to establish forums and topics that foster relationships. In the course shell the teacher can include a forum for prayer requests and praises, a water cooler or cyber cafe to post student autobiographies for student introductions, and a forum for student course questions. Also, students can develop personal homepages with personal information, family pictures, and hobbies. Some teachers provide informal synchronous gatherings online through Skype, Facebook, or Adobe Connect. All of these informal and relational aspects are critical to creating a safe place for interaction and dialog.

7. *Creating small class sizes increases student satisfaction.* A recent study (Lorenzetti, 2010) questioning the value of interaction in online discussion forums indicated that there was a correlation between course enrollment size and online course completion rates. Classes with more than 30 students resulted in students dropping the course, primarily due to a lack of participation by the teacher. The study indicated that larger course enrollment had a negative impact on faculty participation in the course, which resulted in lower student satisfaction (Lorenzetti, 2010). The study also conveyed that larger class sizes resulted in faculty spending less time accessing course activities (Lorenzetti, 2010). It is recommended that in order for there to by dynamic student-to-student and faculty-to-student interaction, an online class should have 14–20 students. If classes are larger it is recommended that classes be divided into two sections for effective online discussion.

8. *Develop assignments that encourage collaborative and active learning.* Since the course instructional assignments are built on a constructive approach to learning, it is important to develop course assignments that foster collaborative and active learning. These assignments are group projects, contextual assignments, case studies, and open ended discussion questions. A recent study conducted with undergraduate adult students indicated that teachers who encourage reflection and require students to relate course content to their personal lives are preferred (Grant & Thornton, 2007). Students also reported that active learning improved critical thinking skills and enhanced their writing abilities. Because of this they reported more self-directed and self-motivated than they thought they were (Grant & Thornton, 2007).

9. *Create balance of student and faculty interaction.* Online discussions are to be welcoming and supportive environments for learning. When developing your course design, there should be equal discussion assigned between student and student, faculty and student, and students to course content (lectures and course readings). This balance ensures collaborative learning between students and teachers and provides a more dynamic context for student-to-student interaction and faculty-to-student interaction. Some students dominate interaction with too many posts while other students remain passive. It is the role of the teacher to address these concerns with students through personal emails or a phone call. This helps to minimize conflict and concern with the student. Also, research indicated that too much interaction in a course can result in student dissatisfaction and unrealized learning (Lorenzetti, 2010). This is especially true when much of the interaction is between students without substantial interaction between student and teacher. Students often get weary reading other student posts that are not beneficial to the course content and materials. The teacher needs to moderate student to student interaction to ensure that students are not spending excessive time only in student interaction. Also, a current study shows that the majority of students interviewed preferred that online courses provided immediate feedback from a teacher who was present, available and organized. Students commented that student-faculty interaction was best obtained through email and discussion forums (Grant & Thornton, 2007). Most students reported that they interacted more with the teacher in the online course than in a face-to-face course (Grant& Thornton, 2007).

CONCLUSION

Effective online courses are highly dependent on the success of online discussions. Since online discussion is the heart of online courses, including both synchronous and asynchronous, then it is imperative that the teacher model effective communication through active participation in the course. Also, the teacher's ability to craft course assignments and activities that enhance collaborative discussion is essential to online discussion. As a facilitator of online discussion, the teacher provides clear guidelines and expectations of online discussion in the course syllabus and in a discussion board rubric. The rubric provides an objective means of evaluating learning through discussion by using the Community Inquiry Model of social, cognitive, and teaching presence. When this model is achieved in online discussions, students and faculty experience the dynamic power and energy of online learning.

DISCUSSION QUESTIONS

1. What constitutes effective online student-to-student and student-to-faculty interaction? On what basis do you ensure that there is quality discussion?
2. What guidelines and expectations need to be established to ensure student engagement in online discussions?
3. How do you balance the three aspects of the Community Inquiry Model (CIM) in your online course? Based on the CIM what are areas of strength and weakness in your online course discussion criteria?
4. What are examples of effective discussion questions and learning activities to develop higher levels of cognitive analysis and synthesis?
5. How do you generate and facilitate online discussions? What are significant characteristics of an effective online teacher?
6. Are students freely deliberating, discussing, and negotiating with others online? If not, do you think it is because they do not feel comfortable enough with each other and the teacher?

REFERENCES

Berge, Z. L. (1995). Facilitating computer conferencing: Recommendations from the field. *Educational Technology, 35*(1), 22–30. Retrieved from http://emoderators.com/moderators-homepage/

Chickering, A. W., & Ehrmann, S. C. (1996). Implementing the seven principles: Technology as lever. *American Academy of Higher Education Bulletin, 49*(2), 3–6.

Chickering, A. W., & Gamson, Z. F. (Eds.). (1991). *Applying the seven principles for good practice in undergraduate education. New Directions for Teaching and Learning.* San Francisco: Jossey-Bass Inc.

Garrison, D. R., & Anderson, T. (2003). *E-Learning in the 21st century: A framework for research and practice.* New York: Routledge.

Garrison, D. R., & Anderson, T. (2011). *E-Learning in the 21st century: A framework for research and practice* (2nd ed.). New York: Routledge.

Grant, M., & Thornton, H. (2007, December). Best practices in undergraduate adult-centered online learning: Mechanisms for course design and delivery. *MERLOT Journal of Online Learning and Teaching, 3*(4).

Lorenzetti, J. P. (2010, September). Is there too much interaction in your courses? *Distant Education Report.* Retrieved from http://www.magnapubs.com/newsletter/story/5339/

Palloff, R. M. & Pratt, P. (2003). *The virtual student: A profile and guide to working with online learners.* San Francisco: Jossey-Bass.

Rourke, L., Anderson, T., Garrison, D. R., & Archer, W. (2001). Assessing social presence in asynchronous text-based computer conferencing. *Journal of Distance Education,* 1–18. Retrieved from http://auspace.athabascau.ca:8080/dspace/bitstream/2149/732/1/Assessing%20Social%20Presence%20In%20Asynchronous%20Text-based%20Computer%20Conferencing.pdf

Xie, K., Durrington, V., & Yen, L. (2011). Relationship between students' motivation and their participation in asynchronous online discussions. *MERLOT Journal of Online Learning and Teaching, 7*(1), 17–29.

APPENDIX A   Discussion Rubric

	Wonderful 5	Great 4	Acceptable 3	Inadequate 2	Poor 1	Score
Grammar & Writing Skills	The student displays good grammar and writing skills.	Most of the time the student displays good grammar and writing skills.	Occasionally the student displays good grammar and writing skills.	The student has a tendency to neglect good grammar and writing skills.	The student is negligent in providing good grammar and writings skills.	
The student participates in the discussion in timely and substantive ways	The student posts to the online discussion 4 times or more times with posts that are on task and contribute in a substantive way to the posted questions.	The student posts to the online discussion 3 times with post that is on task and contribute in a substantive way to the posted questions.	The student posts to the online discussion 2 times with post that is on task and contribute in a substantive way to the posted questions.	The student posts to the online discussion 1 times with post that is on task and contribute in a substantive way to the posted questions.	The student has not participated in ways that are on task and contribute in a substantive way to the posted questions.	
The student demonstrates a knowledge base from assigned texts	The student's posts are clearly built on familiarity with and comprehension of assigned materials displaying higher levels of learning (analysis, synthesis).	The student's posts are clearly built on familiarity with limited comprehension of assigned materials.	The student's posts are clearly built on some familiarity with and comprehension of assigned materials.	The student's posts are built on some familiarity with and comprehension of assigned materials.	The student's posts demonstrate a lack of familiarity with and comprehension of assigned materials.	
					Total Score	

CHAPTER 11

ONLINE FACULTY DEVELOPMENT

Dale Hale
Asbury Theological Seminary

INTRODUCTION

"Training? Who needs training?" "If I'm teaching, what difference does it make how I teach?" Of course, none of us would accept that as a legitimate argument for the absence of training in teaching. On the other hand, we believe we should be allowed to teach as we have been taught.

In an age when terms like "relevancy" have become popular, education sometimes lags behind. However, faculty must be adaptable to survive in a culture that requires them to publish or perish. As Picciano (2001) states,

> Universities may have existed as many as 2,500 years ago, but the modern university has changed drastically during this time. In many ways, it has been a pioneer in the use of communications technologies. The Internet is the result of academicians and scientists working together with government and, to some degree, with private industry to develop and evolve this technology. (p. 110)

Still, many teachers believe they can teach the same online as they do in traditional face-to-face courses. In fact, they would be happy just moving

Best Practices of Online Education, pages 121–128
Copyright © 2012 by Information Age Publishing
All rights of reproduction in any form reserved.

their face-to-face course into an online setting. It is easy enough to video lectures and have the students write papers on what the teacher posted. Once a course is created nothing more needs to be done. Faculty can reuse the same course over and over again. They believe that what works in a face-to face class is will work in an online course.

The issue is not the course content. The subject matter is solid, vetted by the academic institution as not only appropriate but sufficient to contribute to the degree program. The issue is not the faculty person nor is it the student. The issue is the delivery mechanism, how the course materials are delivered to the student and how that student engages and integrates with the subject. It is that connection, the line between the student and the faculty member that must change to accommodate the modality of delivery. Faculty cannot stand up in front of the classroom and deliver a lecture because there is no brick and mortar classroom. The connection between faculty and student must be stronger and more adept in delivering the course materials. Because teaching online is a fairly new phenomenon, helping faculty know how to make that connection is vitally important for the medium and the message to be effective. If educators fail to make that connection, they fail in the attempt to lead the student to the lessons that effectively train them in their field of study. It falls on the educator to be proactive and change how they deliver the message so that it becomes accessible to all students.

What I am proposing is more than just training. To succeed in the online environment, it takes a complete change of perspective. Training implies equipping and practice, as in learning a specific practice. However, if a faculty person wants to be successful in the online environment, a bigger change is required—he or she needs to develop into an online teacher. This kind of development means the faculty are being changed over time, that they are not only acquiring new tools but that they are learning new ways of thinking and being. The dictionary defines "develop" as meaning "to grow into a more mature or advanced state; to progress from an earlier stage to a later stage" (Develop, 1996, p. 511). It is essentially maturing into a different person. While the words "training" and "development" are often used interchangeably, a comprehensive plan that helps equip faculty to teach online must help the faculty develop into an online teacher, rather than assuming they have all the tools and perspectives necessary for their job of teaching online.

If the institution values their students, their faculty, and the curriculum, training will be offered in some form to every new faculty member, whether part-time or full-time faculty. Actually, more than an offer, every new faculty person to the institution should be required to go through the institutional training for online teaching. The reason for this is that every institution is different. The methodology may vary from institution to institution. With this variance comes a different institutional language, complete with institutional definitions and policies that are as widely varied as the institutions themselves. If for no other reason, every new faculty member should go through institutional training to teach online to be aware of the policies that are unique to that institution.

Besides the differences in institutions, the model that drives the particular methodology of teaching in that specific institution may be different as well. For instance, one institution may subscribe to the collaborative model, while another may be based more on a correspondence model where the student is more independent than in the collaborative model. Assumptions that all institutions offer the same experience would lead to disappointed students and faculty. Training helps the new faculty person know the expectations of his or her new institution.

Another reason every new faculty person needs to go through training is because teaching skills cannot be assumed. By ensuring that all faculty receive the same training, the administration can better evaluate each course correctly and give them the "ownership" of the new faculty's teaching. Through the training, all faculty will be given the opportunity and expectation to be "on the same page" as other faculty members in the institution.

BASIC TRAINING

If assuming that all faculty are knowledgeable and accepting of online teaching would lead to a dismal failure, then assuming faculty teach from an understanding of online learning theory must be avoided as well, especially where it comes to the specific institution's subscription to a particular online model. As mentioned above, institutional models for online programs vary and therefore must have a place in the training of all faculty.

If faculty teach as they were taught, gaining an understanding of the more rudimentary methods of basic online teaching would be important. However, rather than beginning with teaching methodology, gaining an understanding of learning theories is an important part of developing good online faculty. Learning theories are addressed in Chapters 1 and 2. Offering students the same format as a face-to-face class makes the faulty assumption that all students learn by the same method. Learning theories provide an important window into the psyche of the individual student who is learning at a distance. Because the online environment is more dependent upon the commitment of individual students to "attend" class, creating course materials that engage the individual learner is important. When the student is separated by space and technology, it takes more skill and understanding of learning styles to design a course that ensures effective learning.

Online teaching is less about the teaching than it is about the learning. However, unless the teacher teaches, the learner is left adrift in a sea of information with no direction or guidance in discerning the most important information. A good faculty development plan will allow faculty to "find their own voice" online and to find the tools that coincide best with their teaching styles. In the initial faculty development phase, faculty should be given the basic tools for teaching online. As they develop skills and knowledge in online teaching, they should be given the opportunity to broaden their teaching approaches and methodologies for effective learning.

In the initial training and development for faculty, the institution's goals and expectations should be expressed in very clear terms. Because these vary by institutions, alerting the faculty to these expectations will allow them to fulfill the institutional expectations. In other words, the faculty can only be held accountable for what they have been given. It may even be a good idea to include these expectations in every contract extended to the faculty members as they prepare to teach their online courses. In any case, keeping the expectations in front of the faculty members from the beginning will help them retain and live within them.

Finally, in this initial development stage, only after the preceding items have been covered should the training move to the institutional learning management system (LMS). If the faculty member is able to grasp the importance of the lessons discussed above, then he or she is ready for the details of course development. Failure to reach the earlier goals, learning how to build a course without understanding the theories and methods behind the tools, would be the same as telling a child to build an automobile—he or she does not have the experience or understanding to perform the task. The LMS is only the transportation for the course materials and the methodology of instructing the student.

DEVELOPMENT: ONLINE GROWTH AND PROGRESS

Once the faculty person has learned and implemented successfully the basics of online teaching, then he or she is ready to learn more skills for effective teaching. First, faculty are given more tools to enhance their online teaching and continued engagement of the student. Second, they become more engaged with the methods of teaching rather than relying solely on the way they have always taught. If the faculty are engaged in the process themselves, a sense of excitement and encouragement is developed about the methods of delivering their course materials in a way that meets today's students, impacting their daily lives so that true "anytime, anywhere learning" is possible. Failing to implement an ongoing faculty development plan will allow faculty to become stale in their teaching methods, harming the message, and in the end short-changing the students' education.

Because online learning uses technology (which is always changing—see Moore's Law below) as a means of delivering course content, faculty must be in a constant state of learning. They are already responsible for staying current in their fields, but now they need to know what methods of delivering course content are available. Having taught with the basic course components successfully, an engaged faculty can begin to develop their repertoire of more advanced tools that enhances the learning of the students. By staying engaged in the methodology, faculty have the opportunity to continually refine their craft as well as enhance the learning of their students.

According to neuroscience, old habits literally die hard. Habits are developed and embedded in our brains with their constant use. Neurological pathways are created and sustained over time by the use and overuse of the habit, whether good or bad. It is easy for faculty to find themselves slipping back into previously conquered "bad" habits and methods of teaching. For example, because lectures can be preserved in either video or written format, a "perfect" lecture can be delivered to the student. However, because of this preservation, caution must be used to keep the faculty engaged in their courses. A lack of engagement by faculty certainly leads to lack of engagement of students. This is one of the harbingers of an unsuccessful learning experience for the student and a dissatisfying teaching experience for the faculty. Refusing to give in to old habits will help faculty remain engaged in the teaching profession through ongoing growth and development of new habits.

Michio Kaku describes the future in ever increasing and astonishing developments. From artificial intelligence to significant change in the auto industry, time will bring about vivid alterations to the way we live today. Kaku (2011) states, "The destiny of computers—like other mass technologies like electricity, paper, and running water—is to become invisible, that is, to disappear into the fabric of our lives, to be everywhere and nowhere, silently and seamlessly carrying out our wishes" (p. 602). Kaku goes on to say that the very word "computer" will cease to be in our language because it will be infused in our everyday lives. If this is true, what does the future of education look like? How will we continue to shape and mold our craft to meet the demands of our future students? The only way to remain viable in such an explosive world is to remain engaged in the learning process. Kaku references Moore's Law (Moore, 2011), which says that computer power doubles every 24 months. Silicon Valley operates with this mantra. According to Kaku (2011), Moore's Law has a finite limit based on the effects of the increase in speed and space (storage space), and this must impact the way we teach. Reliance on the old yellow writing tablet must give way to developing technologies. To ignore them means to quickly become irrelevant in an age when relevancy quickly moves by.

Finally, by remaining engaged in the teaching methodology, faculty have the opportunity to contribute to the ongoing story of the profession, being able to shape and enhance future "specialists" in the teaching field. Living and teaching in a world where the only constant is change means that a faculty who is engaged in the methodology of teaching continues to offer a valuable service to their profession. By creatively engaging the course content, teachers who enhance teaching with future technologies impact their teaching.

CONCLUSION

Yesterday's students were shaped and formed by the faculty they listened to and learned from. Today's and tomorrow's students are having an impact on the faculty and the way they teach. When educational institutions accepted Internet usage as a viable means of both learning and teaching, the growth of the educational industry took on a new tone. Since students have access to such a vast array of information, it becomes important for faculty to know how to guide and lead their students to the best and most correct information. By developing faculty into teachers who can use current technologies, every institution will help shape and mold education for years to come. For the faculty person who will have an impact on future generations is the one who constantly grows and develops his or her craft.

DISCUSSION QUESTIONS

1. In an age of ever-changing technologies for teaching, how does a faculty member remain "relevant"?
2. In the context of this chapter, what is the difference between "training" and "development"?
3. Why is it a faulty assumption to think that a course taught on a geophysical campus could be taught the same way online?
4. Why do faculty need to be trained to teach online?
5. If habits "die hard," how does a faculty member keep from forming bad online teaching habits?
6. Institutions have been known to demand faculty to "publish or perish." How can faculty use the experience of online teaching to either change that model or gain relevant, publishable content.

REFERENCES

Develop. (1996). In *The American Heritage® dictionary of the English language* (p. 511, 3rd ed.). Boston, MA: Houghton Mifflin Company.

Kaku, M. (2011). *Physics of the future: How science will shape human destiny and our daily lives by the year 2100* [Kindle edition]. Retrieved from http://www.amazon.com/Physics-Future-Science-Destiny-ebook/dp/B004FGLX2Y/ref=sr_1_1_title_1_ke?s=books&ie=UTF8&qid=1320893417&sr=1-1

Moore, G. (2011). Moore's Law and Intel Innovation. Intel. Retrieved June 23, 2011, from http://www.intel.com/about/companyinfo/museum/exhibits/moore.htm?wapkw=moore

Picciano, A. G. (2001). *Distance learning: Making connections across virtual space and time.* Upper Saddle River, NJ: Merrill Prentice Hall.

FOR FURTHER READING

Ascough, R. S. (2002). Designing for online distance education: Putting pedagogy before technology. *Teaching Theology & Religion, 5*(1), 17. Retrieved from http://search.ebscohost.com/login.aspx?direct=true&db=aph&AN=5885141&site=ehost-live

Brewer, E. W., DeJonge, J. O., & Stout, V. J. (2001). *Moving to online: Making the transition from traditional instruction and communication strategies.* Thousand Oaks, CA.: Corwin Press.

Retrieved from http://www.loc.gov/catdir/enhancements/fy0658/00065946-d.html; http://www.loc.gov/catdir/enhancements/fy0658/00065946-t.html; http://www.loc.gov/catdir/enhancements/fy0735/00065946-b.html

Chute, A. G., Thompson, M. M., & Hancock, B. W. (1999). *The McGraw-hill handbook of distance learning.* New York: McGraw-Hill.

Demski, J. (2010). Support for online faculty: Two higher-learning networks find solutions that address the needs of both new and experienced online faculty. *Campus Technology.* Retrieved June 16, 2011, from http://campustechnology.com/Articles/2010/01/27/Support-For-Online-Faculty.aspx?sc_lang=en&Page=1

Herrington, J., Herrington, A., Manfei, J., Olney, I., & Ferry, B. (Eds.). (2009). *New technologies, new pedagogies: Mobile learning in higher education.* New South Wales, Australia: University of Wollongong.

Hipps, S. (2009). *Flickering pixels: How technology shapes your faith.* Grand Rapids, MI: Zondervan.

Holmes, B., & Gardner, J. (2006). *E-learning: Concepts and practice.* Thousand Oaks, CA: Sage. Retrieved from http://www.loc.gov/catdir/enhancements/fy0659/2005938636-d.html; http://www.loc.gov/catdir/enhancements/fy0659/2005938636-t.html

Keegan, D. (2000). *Distance training: Taking stock at a time of change.* New York: RoutledgeFalmer.

Ko, S. S., & Rossen, S. (2010). *Teaching online: A practical guide* (3rd ed.). New York: Routledge.

Lowenthal, P. R., & Thomas, D. (2010, September). Digital campfires: Innovations in helping faculty explore the online learning wildness. *Journal of Online Learning and Teaching, 6*(3). Retrieved June 17, 2011, from http://jolt.merlot.org/vol6no3/lowenthal_0910.htm

McLuhan, M. (1964). *Understanding media; the extensions of man.* New York: McGraw-Hill.

McLuhan, M., & McLuhan, E. (1988). *Laws of media: The new science.* Toronto: University of Toronto Press.

Orellana, A., Hudgins, T. L., & Simonson, M. R. (2009). *The perfect online course: Best practices for designing and teaching.* Charlotte, NC: Information Age Publishing.

SECTION III

DEVELOPING AND ASSESSING ONLINE COURSES
AND PROGRAMS

CHAPTER 12

EVALUATING COURSE MANAGEMENT SYSTEMS

Eric Kellerer
Northwest Nazarene University

INTRODUCTION

Whether an institution has had a Course Management System (CMS) for years, or is just beginning a search, the process of selecting a new CMS is inevitable. It would seem to be a simple process, but each campus has a unique set of needs. Each vendor offers a slightly different product, and products evolve rapidly. This chapter will not list the top three companies and prescribe which company is best. Top companies available today might be out of business by the time this book is published. Likewise, new companies will enter the market in the near future. What this chapter will provide is a set of guiding questions that will aid in the search, selection and adoption of a CMS.

PRELIMINARY QUESTIONS

Few campuses are interested in spending money and time on something that does not contribute to their mission. Therefore, it is critical that a

Best Practices of Online Education, pages 131–137
Copyright © 2012 by Information Age Publishing
All rights of reproduction in any form reserved.

campus understand why they are searching for a CMS. What is the business problem that needs to be solved? Articulating the business problem is essential to selecting the right software. In many cases, once the business problem is articulated, an institution may discover it is easier to fix the problem with the current vendor than change to a new one.

There are three primary reasons why institutions seek to purchase a CMS. The first reason is that they don't have a CMS currently. Although the vast majority of colleges and universities have a CMS, it is still essential to know why an institution desires a CMS. Is the interest in a web-based solution that will support face-to-face learning? Wholly online learning programs? Replication of classrooms online? Self-directed learning? All of these are legitimate reasons for institutions to purchase a CMS. When answering these questions, some will be tempted to say, "All of the above" because there is a desire for the software to provide everything. Institutions should avoid this trap. The answer to why an institution desires to have a CMS will guide the leadership throughout the rest of the decision process.

The second reason that institutions begin to search for a CMS is for cost containment. They already have a CMS, but they think that they might be able to accomplish the same for less money. Institutions in this category face a real challenge. If not done carefully, an attempt to contain costs could have unforeseen consequences. The process of managing change on a campus is complicated. On the day before a search for a new CMS begins, faculty on the campus may be quite satisfied with the current software. But by the time a group of faculty has watched four or five demonstrations, there will be several features that become appealing and faculty may now desire (even need) for the delivery of a successful online course.

Although the priority is to contain costs, institutional leadership must determine if there is a commitment to follow through with the change process before the first demo takes place. If there is a willingness to change, then the process should be thorough and every question asked and answered. If the process is not thorough, and the campus decides to keep their current CMS, there will be a percentage of the faculty that will forever be dissatisfied that a change was not made.

On the other hand, if campus leaders decide that they are not willing to make a transition to another vendor, most of this process can be avoided by securing a competent financial negotiator to solicit a few bids from different companies in an effort to pressure the current company into lowering or maintaining prices.

The third reason that institutions begin a search for a CMS is dissatisfaction with their current system. There are no perfect CMS solutions on the market. In almost any change, one set of problems is being exchanged for another. That does not mean a change is not warranted, but it will help if a campus is specific about the concern they have with a company. There are three primary reasons that lead to dissatisfaction.

Vendor Relations

Instructors and students may be quite satisfied with the product they are using, but if a campus is expending tremendous energy or finances in maintaining a relationship with a company, it may be worth looking elsewhere. Perhaps a company representative is not listening to the concerns of the campus leadership or billing problems are causing difficulties. If an institution is facing vendor dissatisfaction, the first line of defense should be to work on that relationship. If the account representative is the problem, demand a change. If billing issues are a problem, work to solve that problem. If the campus is happy with the product, but dissatisfied with the company, it will generally be cheaper and simpler to fix the relationship than to change companies.

Lack of Vendor Support

Another common cause of dissatisfaction is insufficient technical support. If a system works perfectly and is completely intuitive, there is no need for support, but in the absence of a perfect system, good support is essential. Wholly online courses cannot function if the system is down. Students work day and night, every day of the week. A system is needed that will be working when the student needs it.

If the system is unstable and support is not effective, find out if other campuses are experiencing the same technical issues. If others are not experiencing the same problems, a campus should evaluate the cost of investing in more campus resources to fix the problems versus the cost of changing systems. This may include working with consultants to find a solution, or hiring additional personnel.

Missing Features

Finally, there are campuses who are dissatisfied with the features of their CMS. It is important that the pedagogical direction of a course not be limited by the software. However, before making a change based on feature sets, the vendor should be asked to give a written timeline on future enhancements to their product. Assuming it will take at least a year to move to a new vendor, it may be best to wait for an enhancement. If the company is not offering an update that will meet the needs of the campus, another option may be a third-party addition. Third-party software adds a new level of complexity, but it may be an option to pursue that is easier than making a change.

DECISION MAKERS

A relatively small group of people on each campus could easily decide the best software to purchase. Assuming there are two or three people who understand the campus and the challenges of teaching online and at least one who understands the technical issues, a small group could probably make a good decision. The decision is not difficult, but making the decision with only a handful of individuals will almost guarantee a challenging transition and possibly even failure. The purpose of involving a large number of people in the evaluation process is to ensure success in the implementation. People who are involved in the evaluation process are less likely to sabotage the implementation of a new software package.

From the beginning of the process, there should be three groups of people involved. First, there is a person or small group that will make the official decision and sign the check. These are usually top-level administrators. The role of this group is to set the parameters for the decision. Early in the process, they need to set some parameters for a budgetary decision. There is no reason to go through a lengthy process of selecting a vendor the campus cannot afford. In addition, this group needs to set realistic parameters on time-frame. When does the decision need to be made and when should the implementation begin and end? This small group, however, should not be left alone in a room with sales representatives until it comes down to the final negotiations between the last couple vendors. They may facilitate conversations and decisions, but the true evaluation should be people who will use the system.

The second group, the steering committee, is going to consist of eight to twenty people, depending on the complexity of the campus. They are fully invested and understand how the campus will benefit from a CMS. This is the most significant group in this process of evaluation. They will sift through the data, the comments, and the noise and make their recommendation to the campus administrators on what to purchase.

The final group consists of everyone else that anticipates using the CMS. Instructors, students, secretaries, technicians and help desk folks will all need to have a place where they can voice their opinions. That takes tremendous effort, but in the end, information will be learned from them, resisters will have become supporters, and seeds for change that take time to grow will have been planted.

COST FACTORS

Each institution must decide whether they will endorse open source technology or rely on software packages. A chapter in a book cannot answer this question for institutions, but the question must be answered before a CMS search begins. This will help narrow the search. While the question is primarily related to technology, this decision should not be left exclusively to technology leaders. Technology departments on every campus have their own philosophy and culture. There are some that thrive on open source (essentially free) software. There are others that prefer vendor supported products. Whether a campus builds their own software, downloads open source software or purchases software off the shelf, it is essential they understand the total cost of ownership. Each campus should ask these questions:

1. Do we have the expertise to create or maintain a system without vendor support?
2. Is there a user community that can act as user support if our expertise is insufficient?
3. Do we have enough people on staff that can manage the system? Or is there just one person knowledgeable about the system?
4. How many man hours will it take to get the system into a production environment?
5. What server operating system is our staff most comfortable with?

Administrators, along with technology leaders on campus, need to enter into a conversation to discuss these questions and the options before them. There are some obvious strengths to open source technology, but nothing is truly free. Each institution must understand its own abilities and commitment to open source.

FINAL DECISIONS

When a campus has taken the time to list their requirements, it is much easier to narrow the field of possible CMS providers. Whether the requirement list is in the form of a Request for Proposal (RFP) or not, a comprehensive list of requirements should be developed that will be used to evaluate the options. For each feature, a company needs to indicate whether the institution's requirement can be fulfilled within the base package, for an additional price, or only through extensive customization. In addition to a list of features, each product should be evaluated on its ability to grow in scale as programs grow, on the vendors' long-term viability, the ability to port data from one system to another, and on integration with the campus Student Information System.

Beyond understanding the features that are offered, a campus needs to be exposed to each system. Perhaps of greater value than the written response of the vendor regarding a list of requirements, is the ability to experience the system. Faculty, students and support personnel need to spend time with the vendor allowing them to show users how to accomplish the major requirements in the system. If a company representative says, "Yes, our system can do . . . " it is appropriate to ask them to demonstrate it so that you can evaluate if it takes two clicks of a mouse or 57 clicks and a computer science degree. Members of the campus can even ask for a test account so that they can try the features for themselves. A few faculty members should be selected to take real courses and try to build them in a test environment.

A scoring system should be established to evaluate each feature of the system. This will allow each feature to be weighted according to importance and evaluated by the observers. Throughout this process, data should be collected from everyone involved. Evaluators should be expected to give immediate feedback after they see each system.

EVALUATING COSTS

There is a reason that this question appears at the end of the chapter. Although the administrative group will have set parameters for budgeting purposes, it is important that cost not be the only factor or even a major factor in the decision process. It is secondary at best. Many campuses go through the whole process of selection only to abandon their business problem in favor of a cheaper solution.

Costs fall into four major categories:

1. *Purchase Price.* Nearly all software prices are negotiable. Companies need to profit, and they understand that they will gain more from a long relationship than a single purchase. Plan on negotiating the price and note that the best prices can be found at the end of the company's fiscal quarter.
2. *Implementation.* The actual implementation of a CMS can be very costly, especially if external support is needed to import historical data or to create an interface with a campus Student Information System. Before agreeing to a price for implementation, have a written statement of work (SOW) so that it is clear precisely what is offered in implementation and the costs involved.
3. *Labor Costs.* A campus may have several exempt employees working on this project, but their time is not free. Consider carefully what

it will cost to devote employees to this implementation for several months. In the evaluation, include the cost of what will not get done during that time.

4. *Maintenance.* After installation, there will be an annual maintenance or support fee. This is generally a percentage of the cost of the software. Pay attention to whether this is a percentage of the posted price of the software or the negotiated price. Over several years, this could be a significant cost difference. Maintenance costs generally range from 10–20% of the negotiated price. This can be negotiated and may cost less if multiple years are paid in advance.

This chapter provides more questions than answers. If a campus takes the time to answer the questions that are raised here, they will find a CMS solution that will be right for their campus.

DISCUSSION QUESTIONS

1. What is the direction of the campus in online education over the next five years? Is your campus interested in fully online programs? Or solutions to only supplement face-to-face instruction? Or a mixture of these two options?
2. List three primary objectives for purchasing a new Course Management System and rank them in order of importance.
3. Do you have a current Course Management System with which you are dissatisfied? If so, list specific areas of dissatisfaction and what it will take to make you satisfied in each of those areas.
4. Who, on your campus, are the leaders that should be part of the decision making process for a new Course Management System?
5. What is your philosophy, or the philosophy of your campus regarding open source software as opposed to proprietary solutions?

FOR FURTHER READING

Fullan, M. (2001). *Leading in a Culture of Change*, San Francisco: Jossey-Bass.
Heath, C. & Heath, D. (2010). *Switch: How to change things when change is hard*. New York: Broadway Books.

CHAPTER 13

DEVELOPING EFFECTIVE INFRASTRUCTURES FOR ONLINE PROGRAMS

Gregory W. Bourgond
Online Consultant

INTRODUCTION

Online learning continues to grow at a rapid pace. According to the latest Sloan Consortium (2011) report, online enrollments far exceed overall higher education student population by a factor of 19 percent. The Association of Theological Schools, accreditor for graduate theological institutions, continues to accommodate increased online offerings of its schools. Online education is here to stay with a growing number of administrators and faculty agreeing that the quality of online instruction is as good as or better than face-to-face instruction. Institutions offering variation between traditional, web-facilitated, hybrid/blended, and online courses are experiencing the use of instructional technology and distance education practices impacting residential programs. Clear distinctions are becoming blurred. All this is to say that developing effective infrastructures for online programs is no longer an option but a necessity.

Best Practices of Online Education, pages 139–146
Copyright © 2012 by Information Age Publishing

139

STANDARDS

Agreed upon distance learning standards between administration and faculty regarding distance learning principles and practices will ensure consistency, coherence, congruity, and compliance. The quality of offerings will be sustained provided they are adhered to and enforced. Such standards help to ensure there is not disparity from one course to the next and one professor to the next.

For instance, Bethel Seminary's *InMinistry* staff secured agreement with the faculty about the following standards that would be followed in the development and conduct of web-facilitated, hybrid/blended, and online courses.

1. *Consistent communication by residential faculty and adjuncts.* Weekly communication for faculty engagement is vital in fully-distance courses, but also in the weeks which precede and follow Intensives. As such, at a minimum, weekly communication from instructors to their students via email or Announcements in Blackboard is required.

2. *Accessibility to Students.* Faculty and adjuncts are expected to provide regular times throughout the quarter when they are accessible to students. This may be accomplished through establishing virtual office hours in order to communicate and set a clear expectation of when they will be available to interact and respond to student questions. The means by which this accessibility will be carried out is to be highlighted clearly in relevant course documents on Blackboard and communicated explicitly to students.

3. *Regular Synchronous or Asynchronous Communication.* Providing interactive forms of communication is a tangible way to connect with students at a distance. The use of conference calls or point of contact via Adobe Connect are examples of the synchronous and asynchronous technologies that may be used. The *InMinistry* department recommends that a minimum of two conference calls (one at the start of the quarter and one near the end of the quarter) be utilized in order to provide students with an opportunity to connect with the instructor and fellow classmates. Participation in conference calls or in an Adobe Connect session can be optional for students (thus attending to the need for asynchronous forms of communication for many of our students) but may be scheduled as part of the class in order to provide an opportunity for students to touch base with their respective instructors and vice versa.

4. *Discussion Forums.* Use of the Discussion Board in Blackboard is an integral part of *InMinistry* courses. Discussion Forums (not simply "posts") that promote conversations and thorough discussions of

course content are a required part of the curriculum and will be utilized accordingly. Another area in which Bethel's *InMinistry* program developed standards was through consistency in course design, format and delivery.

5. *Course Template.* A course template has already been designed and is currently in use in Blackboard. Though the majority of our faculty and adjuncts currently use this template, from this point forward all faculty and adjunct instructors are encouraged to collaborate with the *InMinistry* department in the utilization of these templates in ways and variations that will benefit their respective course outcomes and objectives.

6. *Video Introduction.* Faculty and adjuncts who teach regularly are required (with the help of *InMinistry*) to develop a personal introduction and course introduction video for the courses they teach. The personal introduction is required at a minimum. A course introduction is ideal. Once developed, the video will be used on a continuing basis, reviewed and updated appropriately. A number of faculty members have already done this and the feedback of both professors and students has been excellent.

7. *Submission of Coursework.* Submission of coursework is to be done primarily through the Assignment link in Blackboard. The Assignment Link in Blackboard is user-friendly for both faculty and students, as it provides an easy way to track assignments that have been sent and received. Submission of coursework via email attachment is acceptable in certain cases. Due to perpetual technological glitches, submission of coursework via Digital Dropbox will no longer be accepted.

8. *Deadlines.* To facilitate the above, deadlines established and communicated by the Coordinator of Hybrid Course Development are to be honored. Established deadlines with regards to textbooks, syllabi submission and course review in Blackboard ensures that courses offered through *InMinistry* continue to meet the highest standards.

Evaluation, review, and improvement of courses on a regular basis is an important component of Bethel's *InMinistry* program. To that end, the following information is part of the consistency required for a quality program.

1. *InMinistry* courses are to be reviewed and updated on a regular basis every two years.

2. Technological and educational resources are to be incorporated into every course taught through *InMinistry*. Such resources include Blackboard, Discussion Boards, Adobe and Wiki technology. Appropriate training, use and implementation in each course will be

discussed and agreed upon by *InMinistry* and the assigned faculty for the course.

3. Training in the area of educational technology—Training of current and new technology and resources will be provided to residential faculty and adjuncts on a regular basis.

4. Intensive courses follow a typical but increasingly "old" pattern: Pre-intensive weeks (heavy on reading), Intensive weeks (heavy on lecture), and post-Intensive weeks (heavy on papers/projects/assignments). *InMinistry* seeks to help residential faculty and adjuncts rethink the ways in which their courses are currently structured and help them envision a way their courses can be redesigned to utilize technological resources (i.e., video lectures, wikis, discussion boards, Adobe Connect) and support the presentation and engagement of course material prior to, and after, the Intensive week. This will "free up" the required contact time during an Intensive week to be used to achieve deeper learning and processing of course material (i.e., small group projects/interaction, field trips, interactive case studies rather than a lecture-only format).

5. Course evaluations are to be reviewed by the Academic Dean in a timeframe that will allow immediate intervention and implementation of appropriate changes. *InMinistry* can choose to seek their own methods of obtaining feedback that will help evaluate the best use of time, technology and structure in its courses. The Academic Dean will collaborate with the Director of *InMinistry* in improving courses identified as problematic through course evaluations and the Director of *InMinistry* will work closely with the Academic Dean to be able to appropriately examine the ongoing quality of the program.

The course standards established above will be relayed to all new residential faculty members and adjuncts assigned to teach a course through *InMinistry*. In addition, these standards will be reviewed and put into practice by current residential faculty and adjuncts. As stated previously, if a faculty member or adjunct envisions a form or structure for their class that significantly differs from the ways outlined in the above proposal, the *InMinistry* department will be most willing to confer and collaborate with them in order to best meet their course objectives and learning outcomes. The standards are intended to provide a guideline to help meet our objectives as a program, not to deter one's creativity in content delivery.

Standards of this sort will prevent misunderstandings, quality disparity between courses, and inconsistency in development and conduct, and they will provide valuable guidance for professors and adjunct faculty.

PROTOCOLS

Every instructional technology used in your delivery system for online learning opportunities requires a protocol to use it effectively and properly. For instance, protocol considerations for discussion forums might include the following guidance.

The best way to ensure full assignment compliance is to allocate some portion of the final grade to satisfactory participation in discussion forums. Secondly, the protocol should declare what is considered a substantive response to a question posed by the instructor or posted by another student. The following protocol was included in a course syllabus:

> Two Discussion Forums will provide a means to address critical principles and issues raised by both the instructor and students. During the course, each student will be expected to make two postings for each of the two Discussion Forums. One of the two postings will be made in response to the discussion forum question posted by the instructor. The other posting will be made in response to any posting of another student. This adds up to four postings, two for each Discussion Forum. Students will be graded on (1) the number of times they participate in the Discussion Forums, (2) the quality level of their interaction with the posted question, and (3) the quality of their engagement with the responses of other students. (Bourgond, 2011, n.p.)

Other considerations might include a demonstration of the integration of what has been learned thus far in the course. In other words, the student must give evidence that they have incorporated what has been learned to date in his or her responses or the answers must reflect knowledge, comprehension, application, analysis, synthesis, or evaluation.

So, in summary every technology used in a course should have an acceptable and approved protocol for its use with the option to expand on the protocol if the objectives of the course or topic require such adjustment. These protocols could extend to use of compressed video, video presentations, audio recordings, postings, podcasts, audio conferencing, various components of a learning management system such as Blackboard and Moodle, electronic portfolios, electronic presentations, social media, survey instruments, Internet usage, wikis, Adobe Connect, or any other instructional technologies used in course development and conduct.

ORGANIZATION

Professors spend a great deal of time acquiring expertise in their academic disciplines. Maintaining professional standards, acquiring and updating academic materials, conducting research and publishing books and articles, and improving instructional delivery is a fulltime endeavor. Expecting faculty to also be experts in the use of instructional technology without instructional technology support is destined to fail. If we expect faculty to walk the high wire of distance learning and instruction, we better provide a safety net underneath.

Perhaps you should consider establishing a Curriculum Production Team, which will provide assistance in the preparation of courses and the delivery of instruction. Such a team acts as a "guide-by-the-side," providing advice, suggestions, protocols, and support developing new courses; revising existing courses; repurposing a course in one format to a distance format; administering a course template; producing video and audio segments; running instructional technology equipment if necessary; or responding to instructional problems.

This team could also provide instructional technology orientations for faculty and students; ongoing formal, non-formal, and informal faculty training and development; and student support services. Partnering with faculty and providing this wide range of support permits the faculty to maintain their academic expertise. Over time faculty gain experience using various technologies and begin to initiate their implementation once they gain confidence and exposure to the technology elements.

A Curriculum Production Team (CPT) might consist of a director who is an expert in instructional technology strategies and conversant in learning theory and styles. The team would also include one or more instructional systems design experts, a production media specialist, a course editor, on-campus intensives coordinator, and a student support services coordinator. Their primary responsibility is to facilitate the instruction and learning of students and support the faculty in the development and conduct of technology-mediated courses. The technology infrastructure maintaining equipment, connectivity, cabling, and providing technical problem support should be handled by a different team altogether.

PLANNING

A matrix support structure could be implemented when multiple course initiatives are planned. Such a structure would look something like the following matrix consisting of functional personnel assigned to specific online projects (Figure 13.1). Oversight and supervision of the functional personnel assigned to each project would be provided by the director of the CPT. Depending on the needs and academic objectives of the course, appropriate personnel would be assigned for each project on a temporary basis until the project is up and running. A planning table similar to the one in Figure 13.1 could be used to allocate personnel and technology resources for active proj-

	Projects		
Functions	**Project #1**	**Project #2**	**Project #3**
Faculty			
Project Management			
ISD Personnel			
Media Specialist(s)			
Student Support			
Technology Resources			
Other Resources			

Figure 13.1 Virtual classroom matrix.

ects such as developing a new technology-mediated course, revising an existing distance learning course, or reformatting a traditional course.

Personnel resources would be brought into the project as needed and when needed during the design and development of the project. Appropriate faculty personnel would be added to the mix to constitute a *tiger* team for the project. Existing responsibilities and faculty loads would be considered to ascertain how much time might be given to such an effort.

In any case, another element of absolute necessity is the importance of having a single office or individual responsible for coordinating and overseeing the institution's online activities—not in issuing edicts or otherwise dictating to faculty what they should put online and how, but as a consistent place where faculty and administrators can go for guidance and assistance on matters of policy and procedure. The design support or student support may be provided in other places on campus, but at least everyone knows that there is one place to go to get answers to questions about online opportunities answered at the conceptual level.

These infrastructures—standards, protocols, organization, planning—will provide a solid platform for online learning programs.

DISCUSSION QUESTIONS

1. What standards exist or need to be developed that will provide guidelines to ensure quality in the thorough development and conduct of technology-mediated courses and an excellent learning experience?
2. What protocols exist or need to be developed that will ensure the proper use and implementation of instructional technology resources?

3. What organizational structure and elements are or need to be in place to ensure the quality of course development or conduct of technology-mediated courses?
4. What one person is responsible for directing the CPT and providing strategic oversight and planning of technology-mediated courses?

REFERENCES

Bourgond, G. (2011). *Ministry Leadership Foundations* (Unpublished syllabus). Bethel Seminary, St. Paul, MN.

The Sloan Consortium. (2011). *National commission on online learning benchmarking study: Preliminary findings.* Retrieved August 8, 2011, from http://sloanconsortium.org/node/184

CHAPTER 14

DEVELOPING ONLINE PROGRAMS

David M. Phillips
Trevecca Nazarene University

INTRODUCTION

The use of Internet technology to deliver educational programs is still relatively new to higher education in general and Christian higher education in particular. Beginning to gain popularity in the mid-1990s (Bedore, Bedore, & Bedore, 1998), the use of the Internet as a means to enable people to complete educational goals has grown steadily and significantly over the past 15 years. Allen and Seaman (2010), in the eighth annual survey of online education, indicate that the number of students in higher education taking at least one online course in the fall grew from 1.6 million in 2002 to 5.6 million in 2009. Based on the 19 million total number of students enrolled in higher education, this means that over 29% of those enrolled in one of the 4,000 institutions of higher education took at least one online class in the fall of 2009.

While most of these online students are found in public and for-profit institutions, the numbers are growing in private nonprofit schools. In 2009, 50% of the private nonprofit institutions indicated that online education was critical to the long-term strategy of the institution, and this is up from 41% five years earlier (Allen & Seaman, 2005).

While online education is a new delivery system in higher education, the concept of making education accessible to people unable to meet in a specific location at a specific time for learning experiences is not new. Over the years, higher education has consistently used various means to make education accessible by taking the learning opportunities to individuals through extension sites, correspondence courses, radio, and TV courses. The Internet provides additional tools and "has the potential to carry all forms of media" (Moore & Kearsley, 2005, p. 7).

This increased interest has resulted in many Christian institutions of higher education exploring ways to enter into the online market and develop online programs. In the initial stages of online program development, an institution must address six strategic factors. The degree to which an institution approaches these factors with a commitment to quality will determine the potential for the growth and sustainability of the program.

PURPOSE

The first step is to determine the purpose for starting an online program. Many institutions consider developing an online program because they see other schools doing it or because they think that this will be a way to strengthen the financial position of the institution (Marx, 2006). Clarifying the reason for venturing into online education is the first and most important decision that must be made. For the program to be successful, the prevailing reason must be that the institution sees the use of online instruction as consistent with and a means for accomplishing the mission of the institution.

As online education began to grow during the late 1990s, the Western Cooperative for Educational Technology (WCET) developed a document titled "Best Practices for Electronically Offered Degree and Certificate Programs." This document was later adopted by the eight regional accrediting commissions and then by the U.S. Department of Education as a standard by which online programs would be evaluated. The first item listed in this document regarding the online program states "in its content, purposes, organization, and enrollment history if applicable, the program is consistent with the institution's role and mission" (WCET, 2011, n.p.).

To develop a strong online program, the mission of the institution must be at the heart of the endeavor, and a way to make the educational opportunity available to more students is necessary if there is going to be a willingness to make the necessary investment and achieve acceptance from the faculty and staff. A clear understanding that moving into online education is mission-driven will help the school move through faculty acceptance and training, create a willingness to do the extra work, and allow for appropriate investments to ensure success.

As a word of caution, it is important to know that while an institution can make money with online programs, it is not an easy way to make money. Institutions that want to start online programs in order to fund other institutional programs will be very disappointed. Not only must schools recognize the need for a significant upfront investment, but schools must continue to reinvest from the revenue to see continued success.

INVESTMENT

After an educational institution determines the reason for beginning an online program, Dunn (2010) states that the next question is, "do you want to have an online *presence* or do you want to be an online *player?*" (p. 9). For those schools that wish to be an online player, the investment will be significant. Even a casual review of the colleges, universities, and seminaries that have entered online education over the past ten years will reveal that the most critical factor in developing and maintaining a good online program is to have an administrative leader who is totally committed to the success of the online program. This leader brings into the operation a good understanding of learning theory, online technology, adult learners, and curricular design principles. Finding such a person will require effort, commitment, and investment. This individual must also be able to coordinate effectively with the administration, faculty, and staff. The schools that look for someone at the institution who has extra time in a current schedule and expect that individual to build a strong online program in the midst of other responsibilities will be greatly disappointed.

While the investment in a quality leader is the first step, a close second is to invest in reliable technology. Faculty and students will demand that the technology not only delivers the needed tools for learning, but has utility quality reliability. If faculty and students cannot know that the technology will work when they need it, they will soon give up. Faculty will refuse to use it, and students will find another school. While some schools may be able to host the online technology, many will find that it is more economical to outsource the technology and pay as they go rather than making a large up-front investment. Finding the right learning management system is critical, and making sure that the educational needs determine the technology used rather than allowing the technology to drive the educational process is vital to full acceptance by the faculty.

Developing quality online curriculum is another significant investment that must be considered before jumping into online education. Current courses, course descriptions, and student learning outcomes can and should be foundational to online courses. However, simply taking materials used in face-to-face classes and putting them into an electronic format will not work. The teaching and learning methods are different in online classes than in face-to-face classes and require a different approach. While the up-front investment can be significant, the good news is that the work done can be used repeatedly over a period of time. Finding qualified course designers with content expertise, online teaching experience, and curricular design background is the biggest challenge. However, as online education grows and matures, there is an increasing pool of people that are capable of online curricular development.

The final significant investment that an institution must make is providing academic resources to both faculty and students that can be easily accessed. This often means adding a number of electronic subscriptions to current library holdings. These resources are becoming much more available and at lower costs than in years past.

BUY-IN

Gaining institutional buy-in is necessary if the program is going to be successful. The initial desire to start an online program may come from governing boards, administration, or even faculty members. Ultimately, each of these groups as well as the institution staff must see the purpose, the value, and the means by which it can be accomplished. Governance and administration is going to be concerned about mission fit and financial implications, the faculty will be concerned about educational quality, work load, and technical support, and the staff will be concerned with processes.

Most institutions find that the most difficult group to achieve buy-in from is the faculty. Until members of an institution's faculty experience online learning from both the student and instructor side, there are going to be basic concerns related to the quality of the learning experience for the student, the degree of one-on-one interaction with students, the amount of time and work involved, and the degree of teaching satisfaction that can be attained.

The process can also become delayed because of the tendency in higher education to run new ideas through endless committee meetings and lengthy discussions. Ogilvy (2006) states that "where business people tend to be action oriented, educators tend to be talk oriented" (p. 22). To get past this he encourages administrators to engage people with "scenarios and to use them to make and implement decisions" (Ogilvy, 2006, p. 23).

Many find that providing faculty with an opportunity and incentive to experience a good introduction to online teaching goes a long way to relieving many of the concerns. Once an instructor experiences a healthy online learning experience, the concerns of the quality of learning is put to rest. The issues of time and work are best handled through clear policies and continual dialog, and the concern over teaching satisfaction comes from experience.

SUPPORT STRUCTURES

While an institution already has many of the necessary support structures in place, it is important to understand the unique needs of online students and to develop new structures to ensure that every student has the needed support. Shelton and Saltsman (2005) stress that to meet the needs of online students it will be necessary to deconstruct the campus student services and reconstruct student services for online students. This includes easy and convenient admissions processes, financial aid, registrations, billing, library, technology, and academic support. They point out that online students will expect "self-service where possible, just-in-time, personalized, with customized and customizable service options that can be delivered interactively and that are both integrated with related services and consistent" (Shelton & Saltsman, 2005, p. 85). Many of those taking online classes will never visit the campus, so all of the normal student service issues must be available to the student electronically.

An important decision to be made is whether to centralize or decentralize these services. It is possible that some services should be centralized and some services should be decentralized. Typically, centralizing services is more efficient, but decentralizing services is more effective. In planning for a successful online venture, a school wants to do everything possible to be both effective and efficient, and sometimes that results in a more complex organizational structure.

Where there is strong buy-in from the various administrative offices, there is greater potential for being effective with centralized services. But if the administrative offices see the new online program as something that is done after the traditional needs are met, then a decentralized approach will be necessary.

ACCREDITATION APPROVAL

While gaining accreditation approval to initiate an online program is not as difficult as it was ten years ago, it is still a necessary process and one that is going to require significant effort and time. Accrediting associations today are very familiar with online education, and while the concerns about online delivery of education being a legitimate teaching method are no longer an issue, there are still concerns that a given institution has taken the necessary steps to ensure that they are capable of delivering an appropriate educational product.

By seeing that the key elements were carefully addressed, the accrediting association is likely to give approval. They will want to make sure the institution has considered the place that online education has within the mission of the institution, the institution has considered and allowed for the needed investment to ensure success, there is strategic buy-in from the critical groups, and they will want to see that all needed support structures are in place. It will also be important that the institution has considered and implemented appropriate policies that address courses and programs (Simonson, Smaldino, Albight, & Zvacek, 2009).

While all other typical academic concerns, such as properly credentialed instructors, appropriate academic rigor, continual assessment and improvement, and accurate record keeping are necessary, some additional issues such as proper state approvals in states where online students reside and processes to ensure that the student enrolled in the class is actually the student doing the work also need to be addressed.

{6}Marketing and Recruitment

Once the program is developed and all of the approvals are in place, it is time to market the program and recruit students. The enrollment return will be directly related to the financial and personnel resource investment made, and this can result in a significant amount of money being spent.

By the very nature of the delivery system, most students interested in online education will already be attuned to the Internet and will likely use the Internet to search for educational opportunities. Thus, a well-organized Internet marketing strategy that includes key word search ads and effective landing pages will be necessary. Creating an electronic environment where potential students can gain all the information they need online, have their questions answered, and quickly and easily complete an application are absolutely necessary in maximizing the online marketing efforts.

CONCLUSION

As online programs were becoming available to students in the late 1990s, there was a sense of adventure and a great capacity for forgiveness when things did not work as planned. Today, online education has become a part of the overall landscape of higher education and students are expecting the technology to be 100 percent reliable, the courses to be effective by design, the instructors to be capable online facilitators, and the learning experience to be meaningful to them. Anything less than this will be unacceptable and a certain and quick death to any online program.

This kind of quality does not happen by accident. It requires making informed decisions based on best practices, sufficient resources for the technology, course design, training, and student services. While there is great growth potential and there are many opportunities to help individuals accomplish their educational goals, beginning an online program should only be done when the institution is willing to make the significant investment needed to ensure a successful venture.

Those institutions that make the necessary commitment to be players in online education will not only have the opportunity to expand their own missions, but will also be a part of helping to provide the education necessary to many individuals needing to work in 21st century jobs. Smith (2010) points out that there "are 40 million American adults with high school diplomas and some college-level training" (p. 12) who do not have a college degree. He also reports that today 85% of all new jobs and by 2014 78% of all jobs "will require some postsecondary education" (Smith, 2010, p.11). There is need and opportunity, but to be successful the approach must be intentional about ensuring quality, and the necessary investments must be made.

DISCUSSION QUESTIONS

1. Over the years many have been concerned about making a college education accessible to everyone. Various methods of distance learning have been tried, some more successful than others. It appears that the method of delivering education using online technology has been the most successful approach to distance learning. What are some reasons why this is the case?

2. In higher education accreditation, one of the foundational concerns for any institution regarding any new program or proposal is that it fits the mission of the institution. Why is it important that any proposed online program be first and foremost a response to the mission of the institution? What is the danger to the institution if it is not?

3. The delivery of face-to-face classes and the delivery of online classes are very different in terms of the curricular design and require a distinctly different approach. What are some ways to help faculty understand these differences and develop online "appropriate" classes?

4. Institutional structure will determine how many of the operational issues of an online program will function. The difference between a centralized approach and a decentralized approach is significant and will determine how many of the issues will be handled. Consider the pros and cons of each approach. How would one approach be better than the other? Are there some items that can be centralized and

other items that can be decentralized for maximum effectiveness and efficiency?

5. Consider the various student support structures that are needed for both face-to-face students and online students. With the necessity of providing equivalent services to all students, what will be the biggest challenges of meeting the needs of distance students? How can an institution ensure that those challenges are met?

REFERENCE LIST

Allen, I. E. & Seaman, J. (2005). *Growing by degrees: Online education in the United States.* Needham, MA: The Sloan Consortium. Retrieved May 29, 2008, from http://sloanconsortium.org/sites/default/files/growing_by_degrees_1.pdf

Allen, I. E. & Seaman, J. (2010). *Class differences: Online education in the United States.* Needham, MA: The Sloan Consortium. Retrieved May 29, 2008, from http://sloanconsortium.org/publications/survey/class_differences.

Bedore, G. L., Bedore, M. R., & Bedore G. L. (1998). *Online education: The future is now.* Phoenix, AZ: Academic Research and Technology.

Dunn, J. I. (2010). *Online enrollment management: Using for-profit best practices at non-profit colleges.* Louisville, KY: The Learning House, Inc.

Marx, G. (2006). *Sixteen trends: Their profound impact on our future.* Alexandria, VA: Educational Research Service.

Moore, M. & Kearsley, G (2005). *Distance education: A systems view.* Belmont. CA: Thompson Wadsworth.

Ogilvy, J. (2006). *Schooling for tomorrow: Think scenarios, rethink education.* Paris, France: Organization for Economic Cooperation & Development.

Shelton, K. & Saltsman G. (2005). *An administrator's guide to online education.* Greenwich, CT: Information Age Publishing.

Simonson, M., Smaldino, S., Albight, M., & Zvacek, S. (2009). *Teaching and learning at a distance: Foundations of distance education.* Boston, MA: Pearson.

Smith, P. (2010). *Harnessing American's wasted talent.* San Francisco, CA: Jossey-Bass.

WCET. (2001). *Best practices for electronically offered degree and certificate programs.* Retrieved May 29, 2011, from http://wcet.wiche.edu/wcet/docs/cigs/student-authentication/Accrediting_BestPractices.pdf

CHAPTER 15

ONLINE PROGRAM AND CURRICULUM MAPPING

Christine Bauer
Northwest Nazarene University

Mary Jones
Northwest Nazarene University

INTRODUCTION

After a Christian higher education institution makes the significant decision to offer an online degree program, success requires adequate administrative and institutional leadership, internal resources, and support from personnel across the university. In addition, essential components for developing a quality online program include program and curriculum maps. The following sections outline steps for creating online program and curriculum maps, which document the learning experience across the program, facilitate the development of a cohesive online curriculum, and serve as a solid framework to guide the design and development of online courses.

ASSEMBLE TEAM

Program mapping should not be an individual effort. Instead, Diamond (2008) asserts a team or committee approach by stating, "...it is absolutely

Best Practices of Online Education, pages 155–162
Copyright © 2012 by Information Age Publishing
All rights of reproduction in any form reserved.

essential for the success of large projects, and therefore the selection of its members should be given careful thought" (p. 76). Diamond suggests the team should include a facilitator (or chair), a department chair or dean, and faculty who will be teaching within the program. Other program development team (PDT) members to consider include students, assessment and evaluation specialists, the registrar, and external stakeholders or in-the-field experts.

ANALYZE ADULT CHARACTERISTICS

To design an online program that meets students' learning needs, it is vitally important to clearly understand the potential learners and what these students need in order to successfully complete the program. Therefore, a PDT should define potential learner characteristics in order to develop a program to meet their learning needs at the program and course levels. What life and work experiences will these students bring to the program? What prior education, knowledge, skills, and attitudes will they have? What are their family situations, expectations, and learning styles?

Next, the team needs to clearly envision what a graduate from the program will look like out in the field. What should a graduating Christian educator, nurse, pastor, or business person know and be able to do in the work setting? What skills and attitudes should he or she have? How will the actions of these graduates reflect university outcomes and ultimately serve in building God's kingdom?

DEFINE PROGRAM OUTCOMES

Program development teams should prepare program level outcomes with student-learning statements aligned with institutional and national standards. The National Institute for Learning Outcomes Assessment (NILOA, 2011a) defines student-learning outcomes as "[those] outcomes statements [that] clearly state the expected knowledge, skills, attitudes, competencies, and habits of mind that students are expected to acquire at an institution of higher education" (Section 1, n.p.). NILOA provides a list of learning outcomes statements which are identified below:

1. Specific to institutional level or program level,
2. Clearly expressed and understandable by multiple audiences,
3. Prominently posted at or linked to multiple places across the website,
4. Updated regularly to reflect current outcomes, and
5. Receptive to feedback or comments on the quality and utility of the information provided.

Based on NILOA's definition of learning outcomes, a PDT should create program outcomes aligned with university, national, and accreditation standards that define what the students should be able to do after completing the program's courses and assessments. Stiehl and Lewchuk (2008a) specify well-designed program-level outcome statements that suggest students should be able to replicate "out there, in the world" kinds of activities. Additionally, they recommend outcome statements to include active statements that identify action or knowledge based learning. There is also a need for demarcating levels of performance along with sufficient rigor to establish assessment. Finally, they assert that there should be an integration with the institution's own outcomes.

One of the most difficult aspects of writing higher education program outcomes is aligning the outcome statements with state standards, accreditation standards, and the university outcomes. In Christian colleges, institutional outcomes may include expectations concerning student values and moral responsibilities, such as *Christ-like character* or s*ocial responsiveness*. In addition, some schools or departments may have comprehensive national and state standards for higher education course content. For example, teacher education programs must adhere to the National Council for Accreditation of Teacher Education (NCATE) standards, state departments of education standards and guidelines, as well as national accreditation standards.

CREATE A PROGRAM MAP

To develop a cohesive online curriculum, a PDT needs to create a program map making explicit connections among courses, assessment and program outcomes. Stiehl and Lewchuk (2005) describe a program map as a graphical representation illustrating a systemic view of a student's planned learning experience within the program from entrance to exit.

According to Stiehl and Lewchuk (2005), program map elements include external and internal stakeholders such as community and university contexts, program or entry requirements, program outcomes, sequence of courses within or outside the program, all integrative experiences like seminars, cohort, or practicums, and capstone assessments. A program map should also visually illustrate connections between courses and cluster courses with similar themes together.

To begin the program mapping process, the PDT needs to establish timelines for the development and completion of the program map and determine the format for publishing the final results of the mapping exercises. These documents could take the form of an Excel spreadsheet, Google Docs, or other online document resources. Using this format, the team should then identify all of the program map elements as defined by Stiehl and Lewchuck (2005).

Steihl and Lewchuk (2005) provide multiple examples of program maps and outline a process to assist program level teams to clearly articulate program outcomes and create a program map. Providing course developers with an integrated program map, prior to beginning the course development process, shows the context and purpose for the online course, while illustrating program components and elements (e.g., institutional/accreditation standards, etc.) to build within and across online courses. This in turn facilitates creating a cohesive learning experience for the online student at the course and program levels.

DEVELOP A PROGRAM ASSESSMENT PLAN

After a PDT aligns the program outcome statements with the necessary institutional, state and national accreditation standards, it is vital to create systems or processes to evaluate, measure, and assess program outcomes. Hence, a PDT needs to identify potential opportunities within the program map for program assessment. The University of Hawaii (2010), for example, outlines how to define and use capstone experiences for program assessment after developing a program level plan. It is essential that institutions define goals and establish learning outcomes. Furthermore, programs should identify where and when learning opportunities will take place. The assessment phase includes multiple stages such as determining the overall goal or objective, collection of data, and analysis and interpretation. Once this is finalized, recommendations for improvement should be used to create future plans.

These university authors suggest that the first three steps are typically done once and revisited as needed, while the last stages are repeated each time an assessment activity or process occurs. The NILOA (2011b) also suggests specifying ways to assess student learning, gathering concrete evidence using multiple approaches for data collection, and developing a timeline for implementation. Ideally, an assessment plan should not be static and must continually evolve. Best practices in program planning suggest creating a multi-year plan where program outcomes and student course evaluations are reviewed each year. If a PDT follows these steps and suggestions, then they will have created an action plan with the opportunity for continuous program review and evaluation.

Quality online program assessment plans also include measurable assessments and rubrics and clearly demonstrate how university and student-learning outcomes are met. In Christian higher education institutions, online programs may encompass complex content and Christian concepts and issues, requiring students to analyze, comprehend, and apply their understanding. Program development teams need to develop quality assessment plans with strategies and rubrics to assess students' performance or demonstration of their understanding of course content and Christian concepts.

CREATE A CURRICULUM MAP

After a program map and initial assessment plan are established, the next step is to create a curriculum map demonstrating how program outcomes are addressed across courses. Udelhofen (2005) defines curriculum mapping as a process documenting how a program's curriculum creates a coherent and consistent learning experience aligned to standards or outcomes that is also responsive to student data and other institutional initiatives.

The University of Hawaii (2011) describes a curriculum map or matrix as "a method to align instruction with desired goals and program outcomes" (Main page), which documents what is taught when, reveals gaps within the curriculum, and informs program assessment plans. This University also cites several benefits in using a curriculum map, which include improvement of communication, enhanced program coherence, increased student achievement, and additional opportunities for reflection. Similarly, Udelhofen (2005) believes curriculum mapping:

> Brings teachers out of isolation and provides a focused, reflective, and collaborative process that has a positive impact on all stakeholders—most important, on students, but also on teachers who benefit from the new collegiality and shared purpose, support, and responsibility. (p. xix)

Essentially, curriculum maps identify where students encounter, practice, and master program outcomes across the curriculum. This reveals how the curriculum supports student learning of those outcomes and identifies needed curricular adjustments. A curriculum map may be completed by creating the following matrix (Figure 15.1), labeling program outcomes

	Program Outcome 1	Program Outcome 2	Program Outcome 3...
Course 1	X		
Course 2		X	
Course 3...		X	X

Figure 15.1 Curriculum map matrix.

across columns and course titles down rows, and placing an X where a program outcome is addressed.

If a particular outcome is not covered by any required courses, a PDT needs to consider dropping it as a program outcome, or determine where it could be covered within required courses. Alternatively, if a particular outcome is covered by all required courses, determine where it should be covered in order to build student success.

On a more sophisticated level, University of Hawaii (2011) suggests replacing the X's to indicate where an outcome is introduced (I), reinforced or practiced (R), mastered (M), and assessed (A) as part of the program level assessment plan.

DEFINE PROGRAM LEVEL EXPECTATIONS

An important but often overlooked decision is defining consistent elements to be used across courses within the program. For example, a PDT needs to define program expectations, such as the instructional philosophy of the program, which includes integrating a case-study approach or incorporating common components for building an online learning community. Moreover, one could include student performance expectations and hours of expected work per course per week, a uniform weekly class structure, and an online course design template that standardizes elements consistently across all courses within the program. Defining program level expectations gives students and faculty explicit standards for course instruction and learning.

DEVELOP COURSE GUIDES

During the last phase of mapping an online program, a PDT translates the curriculum map to the course level by creating course guides for online course developers to follow. Steihl and Lewchuk (2008b) describes "course outcome guides" as "the most basic document for course planning based on learning outcomes" (p. 43). As with a program map, Steihl and Lewchuk (2005) do not recommend one person developing a course guide alone, but rather as a "conversation" among colleagues involving "collaborative thinking" (p. 73).

Synthesizing the work by Jacobs (2004), Hale (2008), and Steihl and Lewchuk (2005), the following framework expands a curriculum map into a comprehensive course guide to steer the development of an online course:

1. Course description,
2. University and program outcomes,

3. Prerequisites (if applicable),
4. Alignment of course outcomes/objectives and assessments,
5. Major concepts/topics/issues/skills to be covered,
6. Suggested course materials and resources, and
7. Evaluation (categories for determining course grades with percent/weights).

Mountjoy and Emerson (2010) provide a comprehensive framework for identifying elements of a course guide. In addition to listing the course description and the university and program outcomes related to the course, they also align course goals and related objectives to possible and required assessment methods. Part of the framework includes suggested course materials and resources, identifying evaluation categories and percentages, and listing important vocabulary terms and concepts.

Providing an online course developer with a course guide developed by a program development team defines the parameters for the course while ensuring program consistency and maintaining flexibility for designing the course to meet program outcomes.

CONCLUSION

Prior to designing online courses, several program level considerations need to be addressed. Careful planning and development needs to occur at the program level to ensure consistency and coherency throughout the program and the curriculum. The process of mapping an online program and its curriculum is an essential, collaborative effort by a team of faculty, subject matter experts, and administrators, with the purpose of developing a cohesive, integrated learning experience for students. Envisioning and capturing the big picture through program and curriculum maps not only facilitates the implementation of consistent elements and expectations during the course development process, but ultimately results in increased student retention as this vision is shared with and experienced by students at the program and course levels.

DISCUSSION QUESTIONS

1. What essential questions should university administrators and faculties ask as they begin the online program development process?
2. Who should be included as members of the Program Development Team?

3. What process will the Program Development Team use to plan, define, and develop the program-level student learning outcomes?
4. How does curriculum mapping process assist Program Development Teams?
5. What are the basic steps to develop a sustainable Program Assessment Plan?

REFERENCES

Diamond, R. M. (2008). *Designing and assessing courses and curricula: A practical guide* (3rd ed.). San Francisco: Jossey-Bass.

Hale, J. A. (2008). *A guide to curriculum mapping: Planning, implementing and sustaining the process.* Thousand Oaks, CA: Corwin Press.

Jacobs, H. H. (2004). Development of a consensus map: Wrestling with curriculum consistency and flexibility. In H. H. Jacobs (Ed.), *Getting results with curriculum mapping* (pp. 25–35). Alexandria, VA: ACSD.

Mountjoy, S. C., & Emerson, M. (2010). MBA Ethics in Management Course Guide.

National Institute for Learning Outcomes Assessment. (2011a). *Providing evidence of student learning: A transparency framework component: Student-learning outcomes statements.* Retrieved June 23, 2011, from http://www.learningoutcomeassessment.org/TFComponentSLOS.htm

National Institute for Learning Outcomes Assessment. (2011b). *Providing evidence of student learning: A transparency framework component: Assessment plans.* Retrieved June 23, 2011, from http://www.learningoutcomeassessment.org/TFComponentSLOS.htm

Stiehl, R. & Lewchuk, L. (2005). *The mapping primer: Tools for reconstructing the college curriculum.* Corvallis, OR: The Learning Organization.

Stiehl, R. & Lewchuk, L. (2008a). *The assessment primer: Creating a flow of learning evidence.* Corvallis, OR: The Learning Organization.

Stiehl, R. & Lewchuk, L. (2008b). *The outcomes primer: Reconstructing the college curriculum.* Corvallis, OR: The Learning Organization.

Udelhofen, S. (2005). *Keys to curriculum mapping: Strategies and tools to make it work.* Thousand Oaks, CA: Corwin Press.

University of Hawaii. (2010). *Assessment how-to: Capstone experiences.* Retrieved June 23, 2011, from http://manoa.hawaii.edu/assessment/howto/capstone.htm

University of Hawaii (2011). *Curriculum mapping/Curriculum matrix.* Retrieved June 23, 2011, from http://manoa.hawaii.edu/assessment/howto/mapping.htm

CHAPTER 16

ONLINE COURSE DESIGN CONSIDERATIONS

Christine Bauer
Northwest Nazarene University

Mary Jones
Northwest Nazarene University

INTRODUCTION

Design and development of quality online courses is a critical investment to ensure the success of an online program, which requires adequate resources and faculty time and talent. Ideally, faculty developing online courses possess content expertise, online teaching and learning experience, and an instructional design background. Typically, however, residential faculty who only possess content expertise are asked to develop online courses as part of their regular teaching load.

For faculty new to teaching and learning online, a change in perception about online course design is needed. Some may believe converting a traditional course to the online classroom simply means posting face-to-face course materials into the institution's learning management system (LMS). However, the online learning environment is different in that simply posting traditional course materials online does not work. In order to achieve

Best Practices of Online Education, pages 163–172
Copyright © 2012 by Information Age Publishing
All rights of reproduction in any form reserved.

the same learning outcomes, course content must be re-engineered. This chapter focuses specifically on course design methods, resources, and best practices to consider when developing quality online courses. The strategies for effectively delivering or teaching an online course are a completely separate topic, which is addressed by other chapters in this book.

GETTING STARTED

While collecting course materials developed for the traditional classroom (syllabus, lectures, assignments, handouts, etc.) to re-purpose for use online can be helpful, many online learning experts agree that designing and developing an effective course requires an understanding of the online teaching and learning environment. Conceição and Lehman (2011) outline several important differences between the traditional and the online classroom, as summarized in Figure 16.1. They assert that the differences have design implications for online courses and for the online instructor's workload.

Differences in how one defines an online course, ranging from a digital correspondence course to a highly interactive online learning community,

	Traditional Classroom	Online Classroom
Space	Instructor and learners in same tangible location	Instructor and learners in an elusive virtual space
Time	A clear sense of classroom time	Flexible concepts of time online
Boundaries	Instructor and learners in one location	Instructor and learners without geographical limits
Use of senses	Close proximity; can see, hear, and touch objects	Need to adapt senses to relate to one another and create a sense of closeness
Level of interaction	Instructor can easily involve learners in discussion and hands-on activities	Instructor needs to carefully develop and implement discussion and activities
Level of course planning	Instructor can add and adapt teaching strategies at the last minute	Strategies must be intentionally planned and designed ahead of time
Cognitive and affective teaching effort	Instructor knows the amount of time needed to focus the mind and emotions for teaching	Instructor may feel always connected

Figure 16.1 Design implications for online courses.

also have significant design implications. Hence, it is important that online programs provide their instructional philosophies to online course developers so that all courses within the program are designed with a similar approach and philosophy of what an online course looks like. As explained in Chapter 15, it is also helpful for online programs to provide course developers with program and curriculum maps and a course guide to clearly demonstrate how the course fits within the online program and what learning outcomes and assessments are needed. In addition, as with online program development, it is helpful to design courses using a team approach, especially if the courses will be taught by multiple instructors (Diamond, 2008).

INSTRUCTIONAL DESIGN PROCESS

Armed with prior course materials and a clear vision of what the online course should entail, ideally a course development team (CDT) is then formed. This team consists of a lead course developer, an instructional designer with online instructional design expertise, and other subject matter experts such as faculty peers who teach the course. However, if a team approach is not possible, then a course developer should independently follow an instructional design model to guide his or her work, asking for peer and online learning experts for feedback and input throughout the design and development process.

The *ADDIE* system, a commonly used instructional design model is composed of the following stages:

1. Analysis—ask important questions about the course,
2. Design—build a framework for the course,
3. Development—create course materials,
4. Implement—teaching the course, and
5. Evaluate—evaluating the course.

Following the ADDIE model, a CDT can approach course design using a systematic, reliable method. The Online Teaching Tips website (n.d.), maintained by Dallas Baptist University Online Education program, a leader in Christian online education, provides an overview of each stage of the ADDIE model. Instructional Design for ANGEL (ANGEL Learning Inc., 2008) also provides an excellent review of the ADDIE model and how it can be used to design and develop online courses within an LMS.

Analysis. During this initial stage of the ADDIE model, a CDT considers the situational factors surrounding the course, such as the:

1. Nature of the subject/field of study—Is the subject theoretical, practical, or a combination? Does it contain convergent or divergent content? Are there important changes or controversies in the field which need to be explored?
2. General context of the course—What are the university, program, and/or external stakeholder expectations? What university/program outcomes apply? What program level considerations need to be incorporated? (Note: these questions should be easily answered from program/curriculum maps and program instructional philosophy.)
3. Specific context of the course—How many credits and how long is the course? Is it lower or upper division? When is it taken within the course sequence? How many students will be enrolled? How will the online learning environment affect course design?
4. Characteristics of online learners—What motivates students to take the course? What are students' prior knowledge, skills, attitudes about the subject? What are their life experiences? What is their online learning experience?
5. Characteristics of the online instructor—What beliefs/values does the instructor hold about teaching and learning? What is his/her attitude about the subject? About students? What level of knowledge/skills/experience does s/he have with the subject? With technology and online teaching/learning? What are his/her strengths and areas of improvement in teaching?

Next, it is critical for the CDT to develop clearly defined course goals and learning objectives articulating what students will be able to do by the end of the course. Course goals encompass broad statements describing what "distinctive educational impact" it is hoped the course will make on students, ideally a year or more after the course is over (Fink, 2003). Objectives entail student-centered statements of intended learning outcomes, which describe specific knowledge (from the cognitive domain), skills (from the psychomotor domain) or attitudes (from the affective domain) students will achieve by the end of the course. Atherton (2010) provides an overview of taxonomies for the three domains of learning: cognitive, affective, and psychomotor. Objectives contain clear, concise, measurable active verbs, and avoid using passive verbs such as *know* or *understand*. O'Bannon's (2008) website contains a method and practice exercises for writing objectives. Bloom's taxonomy is a commonly used framework for identifying measurable action verbs for the cognitive domain, and a CDT should aim for higher levels of Bloom's taxonomy when writing cognitive learning objectives. Churches' (2011) website also serves as a useful resource for identifying digital versions of measurable action verbs based on Bloom's taxonomy.

Design. After identifying the situational factors and articulating course goals and learning objectives, the CDT begins the design phase of the AD-DIE model to build a solid foundation for the course. In particular, when translating a traditional course online, this stage provides an opportunity to rethink the course design. The CDT also needs to be familiar with the university's online course design guidelines, or refer to reliable, external standards to ensure they follow best practices for course design, such as rubrics and guidelines provided by California State University (2009), Illinois Online Network (2010a), Michigan Community College Association (2011), and Northwest Nazarene University (2011).

A critical step in the design stage is ensuring tight alignment between the learning outcomes or objectives, activities, and assessments. One tool online course design teams can use to ensure tight alignment is a course design map, which serves as a blueprint for course design and development and takes a course guide provided by the online program to a deeper level. Essentially, a course design map contains baseline information (such as course number, title, description, applicable university or program outcomes, and course outcomes or learning objectives) and an alignment map (an expanded course schedule designating the themes, topics, issues, or concepts for each unit and clearly aligning the outcomes or objectives, teaching and learning activities, and assessments for each unit).

Bauer (2011) provides an overview outlining the essential elements and characteristics of a course design map. Course design teams need to ensure the course map contains the following characteristics:

1. Ensure tight alignment across all objectives, activities and assessments.
2. Activities incorporate a variety of carefully sequenced active learning strategies to meet various student learning needs/styles, and collectively contain a balance between the types of interaction (interactions between student-to-content, student-to-teacher, and student-to-student).
3. All outcomes/objectives are assessed using a variety of assessment methods.

One advantage of the online environment is that students must actively participate and demonstrate their learning. In other words, there is no back row in the online classroom, and students must perform to show they have achieved the learning outcomes or objectives. When developing a course design map, a CDT can choose from a variety of online activities and assessments to meet learning objectives. There are several resources available to aid a CDT in the appropriate selection, design and development of online activities and assessments. Wor-Wic Community College (2011, n.d.), for example, provides a helpful breakdown of possible activities and assessments according to Bloom's taxonomy. Another example includes the Illinois Online Network website (2010b), which contains an Online Teaching Activity Index page listing multiple options for online activities and assessments.

Another important course design consideration during this phase is the integration of faith, a key distinctive for Christian higher education courses. On his website, Harris (2009) offers specific examples and suggestions for integrating faith into learning opportunities. Shelton, Saltzman, and Bikis (2006) recommend integrating faith as planned and spontaneous opportunities, which requires the formation of an online learning community for these opportunities to occur. Similar to the types of interactions, they continue to assert a threefold strategy for integrating faith online, including course content, the student-to-student community, and student-to-faculty relationships. Course content integration strategies include creating devotionals, designing reflective thinking exercises within lessons, and interweaving Christian principles within the course content. Strategies for creating a Christian student community online include setting up a discussion forum for students to post prayer requests, providing spiritual resources on a web portal, and appointing an individual at the institutional level to organize and encourage the spiritual development of online students. When developing student-to-faculty relationships while teaching online, Shelton, Saltzman, and Bikis (2006) suggest using faith integration strategies such as disclosing personal life experiences and sharing testimonies to bond and connect with online students, and leveraging opportunities to communicate with and minister to students online.

Finally during the design stage, the CDT should also consider instructor schedules and workloads. For example, it can be overwhelming if the course is designed so that the instructor actively participates in numerous online activities and discussions. The team must carefully design the course to ensure students receive individualized feedback using a variety of activities and assessment, without over burdening the online instructor with an unmanageable workload (Conceição & Lehman, 2011).

Develop. Once a course design map is established, the CDT can begin developing course materials. Student accessibility and technical issues need to be taken into consideration when developing instructional elements and materials for the online environment. Ideally, at this stage, multimedia specialists, graphic designers and other development specialists assist the CDT to create accessible learning objects and course materials.

Developing a syllabus for an online course is considerably different from developing a traditional syllabus. Although both need to be learning-centered, an online syllabus also contains more information and details than a traditional syllabus. An online syllabus needs to answer all questions students might have about the course and provide or link to support resources and guidelines to help students succeed online. To ensure consistency and thoroughness for all online syllabi, universities should consider developing an online course syllabus template containing specific sections related to course information, requirements, program level policies, and institutional academic policies.

To compensate for the lack of visual and auditory cues in the online environment, it is critical for online activities and assessments to specify learning objectives, a rationale for the activity, clear and detailed instructions, and explicit grading criteria. In particular, performance assessments should include comprehensive rubrics with levels and descriptors for performance. Issues related to online assessments must also be addressed to avoid potential plagiarism and minimize cheating. When applicable, the CDT also needs to carefully develop objective tests using a test blueprint (Richlin, 2006), scrutinize and revise test banks questions (Driscoll, 2001), as well as build in objectivity for authentic assessments (O'Donnell, 2005).

A variety of approaches can be developed for building an online learning community, such as icebreakers, announcements, virtual office hours, group projects, and online discussions. Many describe online discussions as the lifeblood of online courses; hence an entire chapter (Chapter 10) is dedicated to the topic in this book. Conceição and Lehman (2010) also dedicate an entire book to creating presence online. From a course design perspective, strategies must be intentionally designed and developed in order to create a learning community and presence online.

When creating online content, the CDT needs to consider copyright restrictions, bandwidth issues related to file size and formats, accessibility, integrating technology to engage students and meet learning styles/needs, and incorporation of active learning strategies using Web 2.0 technologies. Course units need to be carefully designed and developed with a consistent, clearly organized navigation structure to minimize the number of clicks required for students to access course content.

Implement and Evaluate. Typically in the ADDIE model, the implement stage refers to teaching the course in order to field test the course design, and the evaluate stage refers to modifying the course design based on the results of the field test.

From a strictly online course design perspective, the implement stage could be also be viewed as the implementation of the course design and the development of the course materials into the LMS. To ensure consistency across all online courses, an institution should consider adopting an online course template that contains consistent course elements and organizational structures. The CDT should also consider developing a teaching guide to assist instructors teaching the online course for the first time, and implement systems and processes within the course design for gathering student and instructor feedback.

The evaluate stage, from a course design and development perspective, could also entail creating a student evaluation plan, a spreadsheet organizing all course assignments and assessments into categories, which are used to calculate final course grades based on points or weighted percentages. Institutional course design guidelines or external rubrics could also be used by the CDT to evaluate the course design at this stage. Finally, a CDT could create a course evaluation plan to identify and evaluate specific goals for course design and teaching, and build in data collection methods within the course design structure collecting student and faculty feedback at the mid- and end-points of the course.

CONCLUSION

Unlike a traditional class, an online course needs to be completely designed and developed prior to using it for student instruction. A team-based development approach can help ensure the online course is consistently delivered and taught by multiple instructors. Although ADDIE is a commonly used instructional design model, it can be effectively used to facilitate the design process for online courses. It is also an iterative rather than a linear design process, so course design teams will likely revisit each stage of the ADDIE model multiple times throughout the course design process. In addition to using best practices for instructional design, course design teams also need address several technical design and development considerations specific to online courses.

DISCUSSION QUESTIONS

1. What essential questions should university administrators and faculties ask before they begin the online course development process?
2. What are the similarities and differences between online and traditional face-to-face course design?
3. When would universities need to use an instructional design model?
4. What types of feedback and data do universities need to evaluate online course design, instruction, and development?

REFERENCES

ANGEL Learning, Inc. (2008). Instructional design for ANGEL. Retrieved July 12, 2011, from http://www.angellearning.com/products/lms/documents/Instructional_Design_for_ANGEL.pdf

Atherton J. S. (2010) *Learning and teaching: Bloom's taxonomy.* Retrieved July 5, 2011, from http://www.learningandteaching.info/learning/bloomtax.htm

Bauer, C. (2011). What is a course design map? Retrieved July 5, 2011, from http://www.slideboom.com/presentations/298130/What-is-a-Course-Design-Map%3F

California State University. (2009). *Rubric for online instruction.* Retrieved July 15, 2011, from http://www.csuchico.edu/tlp/resources/rubric/rubric.pdf

Churches, A. (2011). Bloom's digital taxonomy. Retrieved July 5, 2011, from http://edorigami.wikispaces.com/Bloom%27s+Digital+Taxonomy

Conceição, S. C., & Lehman, R. M. (2010). *Creating a sense of presence in online teaching: How to "be there" for distance learners.* San Francisco, CA: Jossey-Bass.

Conceição, S. C. & Lehman, R. M. (2011). *Managing the online instructor workload: Strategies for finding balance and success.* San Francisco: Jossey-Bass.

Diamond, R. M. (2008). *Designing and assessing courses and curricula: A practical guide (3rd ed.).* San Francisco: Jossey-Bass.

Driscoll, M. (February 9, 2001). Building better e-assessments. In *Learning circuits: ASTD's source for e-learning.* Retrieved July 5, 2011, from http://www.astd.org/LC/2001/0601_driscoll.htm

Fink, L. D. (2003). *Creating significant learning experiences: An integrated approach to designing college courses.* San Francisco: Jossey-Bass.

Harris, R. A. (2009). *The integration of faith and learning.* Retrieved July 7, 2011, from http://www.virtualsalt.com/integrat.htm

Illinois Online Network. (2010a). *ION quality online course initiative.* Retrieved July 5, 2011 from http://www.ion.uillinois.edu/initiatives/qoci/index.asp

Illinois Online Network. (2010b). *Online teaching activity index.* Retrieved July 5, 2011 from http://www.ion.uillinois.edu/resources/otai/

Michigan Community College Association. (2011). *Virtual learning collaborative.* Retrieved July 6, 2011, from http://vcampus.mccvlc.org/

Northwest Nazarene University. (2011). *Angel learning.* Retrieved July 5, 2011, from http://www.nnu.edu/academics/online-programs/e-learning-services/angel/

O'Bannon, B. (2008). Planning for instruction: Writing objectives. Retrieved July 12, 2011, from http://edtech.tennessee.edu/projects/bobannon/writing_objectives.html

O'Donnell, J. (February 9, 2005). Toward objectivity in assessment: Applying the NORMS. In *Pearson eCollege Educator's Voice eNewsletter, 6*(2). Retrieved July 5, 2011, from http://www.ecollege.com/Newsletter/EducatorsVoice/EducatorsVoice-Vol6Iss2.learn

Online Teaching Tips. (n.d.). *Instructional design.* Retrieved July 5, 2011, at http://onlineteachingtips.org/mambo/index.php?option=com_content&task=view&id=73&Itemi=79

Richlin, L. (2006). *Blueprint for learning: Creating college courses to facilitate, assess, and document learning.* Sterling, VA: Stylus Publishing.

Shelton, K., Saltsman, G., & Bikis, J. (2006). Can a true faith-based education be delivered online? *The Journal of Biblical Integration in Business,* 187–202. Retrieved July 12, 2011, from http://www.cbfa.org/JBIB_2006.pdf

Wor-Wic Community College. (n.d.). *Bloom's taxonomy breakdown.* Retrieved July 5, 2011, from http://www.worwic.edu/Media/Documents/Assessment/Bloom %27s%20Taxonomy%20Breakdown.pdf

CHAPTER 17

ASSESSING ONLINE LEARNING

Meri MacLeod
Online Consultant

*I never teach my pupils; I only attempt to provide the conditions
in which they can learn.*

—Albert Einstein

INTRODUCTION

Learning assessment is central to quality online courses and provides important benefits to students and instructors. Students benefit from feedback and accountability that motivates and guides their continued work. Assessment feedback enhances their learning, increases their confidence, and can strengthen their self-esteem as they gain concrete data on their progress and accomplishments. This in turn can reduce the anxiety often experienced by distance students wondering how their work measures up.

Faculty also benefit from assessment practices that review students' learning. When incorporating assessment strategies such as rubrics, grading becomes more straightforward and less time consuming. Communication with students on assignments and grades becomes focused and clear, less redundant and more manageable. Incorporating a variety of assess-

Best Practices of Online Education, pages 173–181
Copyright © 2012 by Information Age Publishing

173

ment strategies provides students with more timely and frequent feedback without the instructor initiating individual feedback to each student. Direct communication from the professor can be reduced, while students receive increased feedback. In addition, assessment strategies such as rubrics and portfolios can have double use as they document outcomes for both a course and program review.

MAJOR NEW INFLUENCES

The expansion of interactive learning centered pedagogies is stimulating new assessment practices (Lombardi, 2007). Research now demonstrates how interactive media can enhance student learning and can expand the types of assessments now possible, while increasing the reliability of the data gathered on student learning (Clarke, 2009; Dede, 1998, 2000, 2007). With new interactive technologies, it is possible for teachers to create online "environments where students can learn by doing, receive feedback, and continually refine their understanding and build new knowledge" (Bransford, Brown, & Cocking, 2000, p. 206). Not only can interactive technology create opportunities for deep learning for students, it has the potential to be used to create multidimensional assessments of complex problem-solving, expert decision making, and collaborative real life engagement as professionals (Dede, 2007).

Research in the cognitive sciences regarding how people learn continues to influence educational practices, including assessment. In an introductory announcement of *Knowing What Students Know: The Science and Design of Educational Assessment,* Pellegrino (2002) notes that, "much of what we've been doing in assessment has been based on impoverished models of cognition" (p. 49). Simplistic, one-size-fits-all tests are inadequate to capture a reliable picture of what students know and understand, reflects Pellegrino. This is especially true as scholars recognize that learning takes place in social contexts and involves active engagement between the learner and what is being learned.

> We make sense of every new experience and every new piece of information actively, in terms of our existing images of the world....We construct our understandings over time, connecting new pieces of information with our existing knowledge in ways that make sense to us. One of the implications of this is that people learn cumulatively. (Jarvis, Holford & Griffin, 1998, p. 142)

ASSESSMENT DEFINED

The assessment of student learning is a process of gathering and reviewing information from "diverse sources to develop a deeper understanding of what students know, understand, and can do with their knowledge as a result of their educational experiences; the process culminates when assessment results are used to improve subsequent learning" (Huba & Freed, 2000, p. 8). Bartley (2006) describes the work of assessment as creating "appropriate, authentic, reliable, and ethical online assessment methodology that measures learning, engages the learner, is integrated into the learning process, and promotes further learning" (p. 17).

Assessment is made up of two connecting components; formative assessment, which occurs during a course or learning experience and summative assessment, which occurs at the conclusion of a learning experience or course. Formative and summative assessments are ideally interwoven to form a continuous assessment environment—each assignment building on the former, with dialogue and formative feedback from one, which then provides the foundation for the next learning challenge, each in turn deepening students' understanding and contributing to the quality of the next assessment task (Morgan & O'Reilly 2006). In this way assessment, as intended, facilitates higher levels of student achievement as a course develops (Pellegrino, 2002). While summative assessment best identifies the cumulative learning a student has achieved, it is incomplete without formative assessment across a course.

In the online course, formative assessment provides added benefits that enhance the quality of a course. First, online learners need to become active in their learning, and formational assessment that involves accountability brings students into active roles as learners. Examples include the use of carefully structured discussion forums, self-assessment reports, and peer-review assignments. In addition, student evaluation of the online environment and course design is critical as instructors gain greater understanding into the factors that contribute to or obstruct learning. Learning and assessment are not two separate phases, but interwoven course elements that stimulate, guide and focus student learning (Beebe, Vonderwell & Boboc, 2010). Macdonald noted that "assessment makes a conspicuous impact on online collaborative study, and can be used to support students in their gradual acquisition of various skills..." (Macdonald, 2003, pp. 381–382). Principles for creating online assessment include:

1. Effective assessment follows a clear pedagogical purpose and is consistent with the abilities and qualities one seeks to develop in students. Weave formative assessment through the learning strategies rather than just using summative at the end. Send a consistent message of what you value in your courses through what and how you assess student learning.
2. Provide a clear explanation for the aims and value of each assessment requirement. Information to students regarding how the learn-

ing task and the assessment fit together with the purpose and value each has in the overall course objectives is motivational to students.

3. Provide adequate and timely feedback to students regarding their engagement in the course and their progress toward the expected learning.

4. Be mindful of the danger of over assessing. While assessment is an important student motivator, too much assessment can develop destructive levels of anxiety in the student.

5. Work to create a valid and reliable picture of a student's performance by using a mix of approaches. Validity refers to "whether or not assignments provide the truest picture possible of the particular knowledge and abilities being measured by the assessment assignments" (Morgan & O'Reilly, 2006, p. 95). Reliability relates to the consistency of assessment marks.

ASSESSMENT STRATEGIES

Rubrics. A rubric describes specific characteristics of what is expected from a learning assignment such as a research paper, case study analysis, collaborative project, or performance. Rubrics identify specific criteria on which the student work will be assessed, with typically three to five levels of distinct quality (novice, proficient, highly proficient). Rubrics provide clarification and specific information to students on how their work will be assessed. They help refine instructional and assessment outcomes for faculty, and they can illustrate to students and stakeholders the desired growth expected. In the online environment rubrics can provide a valuable venue for discussion and feedback to students (Dornisch & McLoughlin, 2006; Gaytan & McEwen, 2007). Rubrics convey to learners "how their work compares to a standard, the consequences of remaining at their current level of skill or knowledge, as well as information about how to improve" (Huba & Freed, 2000, p. 154).

Rubrics contain two main components: specific *criteria*, which are categories of skills on which a student's work (performance or artifact/product) will be evaluated, and *levels of quality* of the work (excellent, satisfactory) that are assessed for each criteria (Dornisch & McLoughlin, 2006). Cal State Fresno (2010) provides the following sequence for creating rubrics:

1. Identify what you are assessing (e.g., critical thinking).
2. Identify the characteristics of what you are assessing (e.g., appropriate use of evidence, recognition of logical fallacies).
3. Describe the best work you could expect using these characteristics. This describes the top category which you may label "exemplary" or "outstanding".

4. Describe the worst acceptable work using these characteristics. This describes the lowest acceptable category.
5. Describe an unacceptable work by a student. This describes the lowest category.
6. Develop descriptions of intermediate-level work and assign them to intermediate categories. You might decide to develop a scale that runs from 1 to 5 (unacceptable, marginal, competent, very competent, outstanding), from 1 to 3 (novice, competent, exemplary), or any other set that is meaningful.

Guidelines for using rubrics include:

1. Provide the rubric with the assignment so students will know how their work will be graded.
2. Use the rubric when grading, return the rubric with the graded work, and rather than writing extensive comments on the student work, simply highlight relevant segments of the rubric.
3. Develop a rubric with students for an assignment or group project. Students can then monitor themselves and their peers using agreed-upon criteria that they assisted in developing.

COLLABORATIVE ASSESSMENTS

Collaborative assignments that involve interaction are an important component of online courses. These types of assignments keep students engaged and have the potential to broaden learning to include vital skills and deeper understanding in areas such as problem solving, team work, group decision making, managing multifaceted projects and deadlines, and negotiation with individuals who hold different points of view (Morgan & O'Reilly, 2001). Integrating assessment for both individual and group work is important to gain high levels of student collaboration. Unlike a face-to-face classroom, online collaboration can provide transcript records of student interaction, which makes participation explicit and easier to assess. Effective collaborative assignments include a common goal, shared responsibility, mutual dependence for the outcome of the work together, and the required need to reach shared agreement (Oliver, Herrington, Herrington & Reeves, 2007).

Assessment of a collaborative assignment can include the review of periodic online meetings, the review of a project wiki, and the summative review of the final project. Assessment of individual student participation and the group work as a whole conveys the value of both components. Macdonald (2003) noted that "assessment makes a conspicuous impact on online collaborative study, and can be used to support students in their gradual acquisition of various skills" (p. 381). Collaborative assignments and integrated assessment provide an opportunity to nurture godly attitudes and behaviors when working with others, such as the demonstration of mutual respect, patience and the inclusion of others.

Recommendations for effective online collaborative learning include:

1. Be alert to the quality of communication skills students demonstrate and the degree of relational community within the class. Consider if trust building or skill development assignments may be needed before the groups are able to work collaboratively together.

2. Be cautious of how much transcript data to include in assessment decisions. Select representative samples in order to manage the volume of assessment data. Review the data with a rubric for efficient use of time and consistency.

3. Combine student self-assessment and peer assessment with instructor assessment in order to gain a complete picture of how the collaboration within the groups occurred.

4. Use an assessment rubric designed for collaboration (a sample is available at the author's website: www.digitalseminarian.com/resources) so students are clear regarding the criteria on which they will be assessed for their collaborative work. Invite student feedback on the rubric at the conclusion of the assignment and review for ambiguity and appropriate completeness.

5. Be alert to how the group is functioning as they progress through the assignment. Look for evidence of purposeful dialogue, respectful communication, and collaborative decision-making. Guide and coach as needed.

6. Be clear regarding the weight given to individual work and group work. The weight distribution needs to be consistent with the desired learning objectives, such as 30% for individuals and 70% for the group as a whole.

PEER REVIEW

Peer review assessments guide students in reflecting and providing feedback to their peers. Assignments that include peer review need to be sufficiently complex so students can make revisions in their work with the aid of feedback from their peers. Students submit a draft of their work to a small group of peers, and each peer responds with feedback based on guidelines provided through a rubric. Each student reflects on feedback received and determines how to incorporate it in their next revision (Hickman, Bielema,

& Gunderson, 2006). Often students find giving feedback to peers difficult. When using peer review, begin with a rubric and samples of feedback on student work. Coach students so they know what to look for in the assignment and how to convey their ideas. A summative assessment on the assignment needs to include documentation of all feedback a student received and how it was incorporated in the final project.

SELF REFLECTION

Across the assessment literature, whether for face-to-face or online courses, self-reflective assessment is a growing practice. As faculty gain greater insight into how students learn, there is a deepening value for the place critical reflection plays. The inclusion of self-reflective evaluations with any assessment strategy can deepen student learning. Consider asking students to reflect on how they prepared and carried out a challenging assignment and what they discovered about themselves though the process. Another example of a self-reflection assignment conducted annually over the length of a degree program can be found at the Digital Seminarian website. This proved to be a very valuable experience for the students, who gained important self-awareness and developed the habit of reflecting on their personal growth. Additionally, the assessment made a valuable contribution to the program review for accreditation approval. Journaling online through a wiki or other tool is a self-reflection assignment increasingly more popular.

EMERGING ASSESSMENT TRENDS

Learning-centered pedagogies have become more prominent in the practices of educators, whether online or face-to-face. These include situated learning, interactive learning, problem-based learning, and project-based learning (Oliver, Herrington, & Reeves, 2002; Lombardi, 2007). These pedagogies engage students with complex assignments that reflect real world situations. Consider a web-based environment where students learn business communication skills by accepting temporary employment in a virtual recording company. They are given a complex task to complete, and in order to do it, they make appointments and keep a diary, interview the director and employees, and write letters, memos, and reports (Oliver, Herrington, & Reeves, 2002). Another example of situated learning for mission students can be found online at the Digital Seminarian website.

As faculty adopt various inquiry-based pedagogies, new assessment models follow, and two are becoming more prominent. First, authentic assessments allow students to work under similar conditions with similar materials as they might encounter in a real world settings. Simulations, immersive virtual reality such as Second Life, and real world case studies are examples of authentic assessments. e-Portfolios, a second emerging model of assessments, allow students to demonstrate progress over time through the digital collection of iterative and complex work (Palloff & Pratt, 2009). Educators familiar with online portfolios urge the inclusion of student reflections (Brandes & Boskie, 2008). Virginia Tech and Indiana University are leaders in the area of portfolio assessment and make a number of resources available on their websites.

DISCUSSION QUESTIONS

1. Review your course(s) and identify assignments where online students seemed confused and needed clarification. Draft a rubric and test it for these assignments. Refine it after the first use.
2. Take an inventory of your online courses to identify your use of formational assessment. When and in what way do you use formative assessment? At what points in your courses could this resource tool, if incorporated, enhance student learning?

REFERENCES

Bartley, J. (2006). Assessment is as assessment does: A conceptual framework for understanding online assessment and measurement. In S .L. Howell & M. Hricko (Eds.), *Online assessment and measurement: Foundations and challenges* (pp. 1–45). Hershey, PA: Idea Group.

Beebe, R. S., Vonderwell, S., & Boboc, M. (2010). Emerging patterns in transferring assessment practices from F2f to online environments. *Electronic Journal of e-Learning, 8*(1), 1–12.

Brandes, G. & Boskie, N. (2008). EPortfolio: From description to analysis. *International Review of Research in Open and Distance Learning, 9*(2), 1–17.

Bransford, J., Brown, A., & Cocking, R. (2000). *How people learn: Brain, mind, experience, and school.* Washington, DC: National Academy Press.

Cal State Fresno. (2010). *Institutional assessment, research, and planning.* Retrieved July 8, 2011, from http://www.csufresno.edu/irap/assessment/rubric.shtml

Clarke, J. (2009). *Studying the potential of virtual performance assessments for measuring student achievement in science.* Paper presented at the Annual meeting of the American Educational Research Association, San Diego, CA.

Dede, C. (1998). *Six challenges for educational technology.* Retrieved June 30, 2011, from http://www.virtual.gmu.edu/pdf/ASCD.pdf

Dede, C. (2000). Emerging influences of information technology on school curriculum. *Journal of Curriculum Studies, 32*(2), 281–303.

Dede, C. (2007). Reinventing the role of information and communications technologies in education. *Yearbook of the National Society for the Study of Communications Technology in Education, 106*(2), 11–38.

Dornisch, M., & McLoughlin, A. (2006, March). Limitations of web-based rubric resources: Addressing the challenges. *Practical Assessment, Research & Evaluation, 11*(3). Retrieved May 16, 2011, from http://pareonline.net/pdf/v11n3.pdf

Gaytan, J., & McEwen, B. (2007). Effective online instructional and assessment strategies. *The American Journal of Distance Education, 21*(3), 117–132.

Hickman, C., Bielema, C., & Gunderson, M. (2006). Challenges in the design, development, and delivery of online assessment and evaluation. In S. L. Howell & M. Hricko (Eds.), *Online assessment and measurement: Foundations and challenges* (pp. 1–45). Hershey, PA: Idea Group.

Huba, M., & Freed, J. (2000). *Learner-centered assessment on college campuses: Shifting the focus from teaching to learning.* Boston, MA: Allyn and Bacon.

Jarvis, P., Holford, J., & Griffin, C. (1998). *The theory and practice of learning.* London: Kogan Page.

Lombardi, M. (2007). *Authentic learning for the 21st century: An overview.* Retrieved June 24, 2011, from www.educause.edu/ELI/AuthenticLearningforthe21st-Cen/156769

Macdonald, J. (2003). Assessing online collaborative learning: Process and product. *Computers & Education, 40*, 377–391.

Morgan, C., & O'Reilly, M. (2001). Innovations in online assessment. In F. Lockwood & A. Gooley (Eds.), *Innovation in open & distance learning: Successful development of online and web-based learning* (pp. 179–188). London: Routledge.

Morgan, C., & O'Reilly, M. (2006). Ten key qualities of assessment online. In S. L. Howell & M. Hricko (Eds.), *Online assessment and measurement: Foundations and challenges* (pp. 86–101). Hershey, PA: Idea Group.

Oliver, R., Herrington, J., & Reeves, T. (2002). *Authentic activities and online learning.* Paper published in Quality Conversations, Proceedings of the 25th HERDSA Annual Conference, Perth, Western Australia.

Oliver, R., Herrington, J., Herrington, A., & Reeves, T. (2007). Representing authentic learning designs supporting the development of online communities of learners. *Journal of Learning Design, 2*(2). Retrieved June 30, 2011, from http://www.jld.qut.edu.au/publications/vol2no2/documents/Oliveretal JLDVol2No2.pdf

Palloff, R., & Pratt, K. (2009). *Assessing the online learner: Resources and strategies for faculty.* San Francisco: Jossey-Bass.

Pellegrino, J. (2002, Winter). Knowing what students know. *Issues in Science and technology, XIX*(2). Retrieved June 16, 2011, from http://www.uic.edu/depts/oaa/genedconv/pellegrinoissues.pdf

ABOUT THE EDITORS

Mark A. Maddix, Ph.D. is Dean of the School of Theology and Professor of Christian Education at Northwest Nazarene University (NNU). He developed and launched the first fully online Master of Arts degree in Spiritual formation at NNU. Since then he has developed seven masters' degrees including a fully online Master of Divinity degree and online undergraduate degree in Christian Ministries. He has conducted online faculty development at several Universities and Seminaries around the world.

Dr. Maddix serves as the President of the North American Professors of Christian Education (NAPCE) and is a member of the Wesleyan Theological Society (WTS), the Society for the Study of Psychology and Wesleyan Theology (SSPWT), and Religious Education Association (REA). He has published over thirty book chapters and academic articles in a variety of journals including the *Christian Education Journal, Journal of Christian Education and Information Technology* (Korea), *Wesleyan Theological Journal, The Journal of Religious Education, Evangelical Journal,* and *Didache.* He is the coauthor of *Discovering Discipleship: Dynamics of Christian Education* and co-edited *Spiritual Formation: A Wesleyan Paradigm,* and *Pastoral Perspectives: A Wesleyan Paradigm.*

Dr. Maddix is a frequent speaker in the areas of Christian discipleship, Spiritual formation, Wesleyan theology, and online education. He has taught at over 20 college and seminaries around the world. His wife Sherri is a registered nurse and they have two adult children, Adrienne Maddix Meir and Nathan Maddix.

Best Practices of Online Education, pages 183–185
Copyright © 2012 by Information Age Publishing
All rights of reproduction in any form reserved.

James R. Estep, Ph.D. was raised in Lexington, Kentucky where he was an active member of the Southern Acres Christian Church. Jim has always had a keen interest in Christian education, and this has developed into a passion for the subject. He holds memberships in the North American Professors of Christian Education (NAPCE), Religious Education Association (REA), the Evangelical Theological Society (ETS), and is an active participant with the Stone-Campbell Journal Conference. His students nominated him five times to Who's Who among America's Teachers.

He has presented papers and conducted workshops at the North American Christian Convention, Stone-Campbell Journal Conference (formerly Fellowship of Professors), National Youth Leader's Conference, Childhood Spirituality Conference, E.T.S. Midwest Regional meeting, and the annual meetings of the North American Professors of Christian Education, Association on Biblical Higher Education (formerly the Accrediting Association of Bible Colleges), the Higher Learning Commission of the North Central Association, and the Evangelical Theological Society. He has also contributed articles and reviews to *Christian Standard, Encounter, Restoration Quarterly, Leaven, Christian Education Journal, Religious Education, Lexington Theological Quarterly, Journal of Christian Education and Information Technology* (Korea), *The Near East Archaeological Bulletin,* and *Stone-Campbell Journal* on Christian Education and related subjects. He has served as contributing editor on six different books. Jim serves as the coordinator of the Christian Education Study Group at SCJC and on the editorial board of *Biblical Higher Education Journal* (ABHE), as well as served as an article/book editor and special edition (Fall 2012) editor for *Christian Education Journal.* He was likewise a four-time contributor to the Lily funded NAPCE web-based project "20th Century Christian Educators." Jim has also co-authored/edited eight books, published by College Press, Broadman & Holman, and Wifp & Stock.

Dr. Estep and his wife Karen (Ph.D., Michigan State University) have three children: Dylan, Dovie, and Budd. Jim enjoys time with his family, research and writing, spending time with his children, science fiction (more specifically *anything* Star Trek), and the company of friends in bookstores (particularly *used*) and/or coffee shops (particularly Starbucks).

Mary E. Lowe, Ed.D. grew up in Haiti as the daughter of missionaries and learned firsthand about Theological Education by Extension. She serves as Dean of the Virtual Campus at Erskine Seminary and is working to provide theological education online to those who live locally and globally. Lowe is the Executive Director of ACCESS, the Association for Christian Distance Education.

Mary's professional interest is spiritual formation. She along with her husband, Dr. Steve Lowe, co-directed the National Consultation on Spiritual Formation in Theological Distance Education funded by the Wabash

Center for Teaching and Learning. The results of that consultation have been published in the *Christian Education Journal.* Another area of interest is leadership development for women. Lowe's article *Breaking the stained glass ceiling: Women's collaborative leadership style as a model for theological education* will be published in early 2012. She and her husband live in Due West, South Carolina.

ABOUT THE CONTRIBUTORS

Jay Richard Akkerman, D.Min. is director of graduate theological online education at Northwest Nazarene University. Presently he directs nine fully online Master of Divinity and Master of Arts programs in the School of Theology and Christian Ministries, including programs in Christian Education; Missional Leadership; Pastoral Ministry; Spiritual Formation; and Youth, Church & Culture.

As an associate professor of pastoral theology, Dr. Akkerman also teaches on NNU's undergraduate campus in Nampa, Idaho. An ordained minister in the Church of the Nazarene, Dr. Akkerman had extensive pastoral experience prior to joining NNU's faculty. He and his wife Kim live in Nampa with their three daughters.

Jason D. Baker, Ph.D. is a professor of education at Regent University and the advisor of the distance education cognate in the Doctor of Education program. He previously worked as an educational consultant at Loyola College in Maryland where his efforts included training faculty on instructional technology, administering the internal technical training program, and managing the college's Web presence. He has authored and edited numerous books and articles related to online learning and educational technology and consulted with numerous organizations regarding the development and management of developing online learning programs. He also manages Baker's Guide to Christian Online Learning, the leading website dedicated to Christian distance education, at www.BakersGuide.com.

Best Practices of Online Education, pages 187–193
Copyright © 2012 by Information Age Publishing
All rights of reproduction in any form reserved.

Christine Bauer, Ph.D. received her doctoral degree in education with an emphasis in Instructional Design for Online Learning from Cappella University in 2003 and has been involved with online learning since 1995. Christine began her career in education teaching with technology at the middle and high school level and since served in various roles related to curriculum and professional development.

Currently Christine serves as the E-Learning Director at Northwest Nazarene University in Nampa, Idaho, providing institutional leadership to the academic development of the University's distance learning offerings, and consults with faculty developing and teaching online and blended courses.

Prior to NNU she served as the Curriculum Director at the Idaho Digital Learning Academy, a state-sponsored online secondary school. In addition to presenting at conferences around the country, over the years Christine has facilitated numerous workshops for hundreds of K–20 teachers related to effectively integrating technology into the classroom, and using instructional design methods and best practices for designing and developing online and blended courses.

Greg Bourgond, D.Min, Ed.D. earned a bachelor's degree in Psychology from Chapman University (1979), a Master of Divinity degree (M.Div.) from Bethel Seminary in San Diego (1983), a Doctor of Ministry degree (D.Min.) in Church Leadership from Bethel (1997), and an Ed.D. in Instructional Technology and Distance Education (2001) from Nova Southeastern University. He completed post-graduate studies in the Institute for Educational Management at Harvard Graduate School of Education (2003). He is the author of "A Rattling of Sabers: Preparing Your Heart for Life's Battles" published in 2010 and "Papa's Blessings: The Gift That Keeps Giving" published in 2011.

He most recently served as Assistant to the Provost of Bethel University and Director of Strategy for Online Education providing direction for advancement of online education across Bethel University four academic units; College of Arts and Sciences, College of Professional and Adult Studies, Graduate School, and the Seminary. He provided operational support to Bethel Seminary in the areas of distributed learning, budget development, and future strategic operations. He has also served as Vice President for Operations and Strategic Initiatives, Dean for the Center of Transformational Leadership, and Dean of Academic Affairs and Instructional Technology at Bethel Seminary with transregional responsibilities in its six teaching locations, four on the eastern seaboard, one in San Diego, and the main campus in St. Paul, Minnesota.

Greg is currently the senior associate pastor of Christ Community Church in Rochester and also serves as a consultant and teacher in the areas of leadership formation and development, spiritual and personal formation, legacy, organizational systems theory and applications, strategic planning, distance learning and technology-mediated course delivery, and small group dynamics. He is the President and Founder of Heart of a Warrior Ministries, a ministry dedicated to helping men live lives of integrity and honor under the authority of God. He has taught many schools, churches, and organizations. Greg has been happily married for 42 years and enjoys his six grandchildren every chance he gets.

Robert Dale Hale, Ph.D. has served as Director of Distributed Learning at Asbury Theological Seminary since 2004. Dale directs the online program and the distance learning classes that link Asbury's Kentucky campus with their Florida Dunnam campus. He also provided guidance to the seminary through the change from a proprietary learning management system to the open source learning management system, Moodle.

Before coming to Asbury seminary he pastored two congregations, one located in Ponca City, Oklahoma, and Council Bluffs, Iowa. Pastoring those two churches created a passion for equipping the church with both well-trained pastors and a laity well-versed in understanding of the scriptures. It is this passion for pastor and laity that drives his commitment to a quality online program for Asbury Theological Seminary.

Sensing God's call on his life for further education, Dale entered seminary in 1993. He graduated with a dual degree, the MDiv from Asbury Theological Seminary and the MSW from the University of Kentucky. Since then, Dale completed the PhD in Higher Education from the University of Kentucky and was hired into the position he currently holds with Asbury. Dale is also an affiliate faculty for Asbury, teaching mainly in the Christian Discipleship area. He and his wife live just outside of Wilmore on five acres.

Mark H. Heinemann, Ph.D. serves as professor of Christian education at Dallas Theological Seminary. Before coming to Dallas he served in campus ministry and the pastorate, as well as over 10 years as lecturer in Practical Theology at a German seminary. While in Germany he served for three years as a consultant to various European Bible schools and seminaries. His writings include several articles about online theological education.

Mary Jones, Ph.D. is Associate Professor and Director of the Online Teaching and Learning Graduate Program at Northwest Nazarene University. For the past twelve years she has developed online curriculum and taught undergraduate and graduate education courses in online learning environments. She is currently developing the education curriculum for a new online graduate program emphasis in Online Teaching. The program will prepare K12 elementary and secondary teachers with skills they need to facilitate and teach in virtual classrooms.

Eric Kellerer, Ed.D. is currently the Executive Director of Information Technology at Northwest Nazarene University (NNU). During his tenure at NNU, Eric Kellerer has been instrumental in building a solid technology infrastructure to support education in the classroom as well as online learning. When he came to the University in 1997, the annual technology budget was just over $200,000 and distant education was only a dream. Today, the Information Technology budget is $1.4 million and NNU offers 5 graduate, 1 undergraduate degree and 1 certification program fully online in 14 different programs to over 600 students. In addition to his role in technology, Kellerer is involved as a faculty member in strategic campus decisions.

Kellerer received his Ed.D. degree in Curriculum and Instruction with an emphasis on technology in distance education. The title of Kellerer's dissertation was "Internet-based, asynchronous connected learning and the role of course management software." In the dissertation, the author explored pedagogical practices and the use of software in online learning.

In addition to his role with technology, Kellerer serves as the Director of International Relations. In this role, Kellerer is responsible for developing relationships that promote the recruiting of international students as well as opportunities for NNU to send students to cross-cultural experiences in other countries.

Steve Kemp, Ph.D. is the founding Academic Dean of the Antioch School of Church Planting and Leadership Development, the first truly church-based and competency-based higher education institution to receive CHEA-recognized accreditation. He also serves as Director of Institutional Partnerships for BILD International, the parent organization of the Antioch School, through which he helps other academic and mission institutions to include nonformal, in-service, church-based training in their programs. Additionally, he serves as a Pastor of the Ames/Des Moines City Church, a network of churches in Central Iowa. Previously, Kemp served as Vice-President and Dean of External Studies (distance education) for Moody Bible Institute, as well as Associate Dean of Nontraditional and Distance Education for Trinity Evangelical Divinity School.

He has contributed a recent article in Christian Education Journal called *Situated Learning: Optimizing God-Given Learning Communities* in which he tries to help both traditional campus and non-traditional off-campus programs make better use of the primary social relationships of students. This contribution flows from his major doctoral research and dissertation titled "Experiential Learning and the Role of Primary Social Relationships as Contexts for Situated Learning in Distance Education Courses of Evangelical Theological Education Institutions," building on his earlier monograph called "Learning Communities in Distance Education." Kemp has served in various leadership positions of ACCESS, the Christian distance education association, and been active in many professional capacities, such as the Criteria Review Committee that rewrote the current accreditation standards for the Association of Biblical Higher Education. He has taught more than 130 online courses and more than 1300 students.

Kemp is married to Judy whose graduate education is in traditional university student services. He has two emerging adult children, Michael 19 and Sarah 17, who keep him sharp. The Kemps live in Ames, Iowa with their brown mini-dachshund named Mack, but host many others through weekly house church events, football tailgate parties, and other short- and long-term guests who stay with them for training and events associated with BILD International or their church.

Stephen D. Lowe, Ph.D. has served in Christian higher education since 1984 teaching both at the undergraduate and graduate levels through both on campus and online education. His degrees in Bible, theology, and education have had an integrative influence on his teaching, research, and writing. He and his wife, Dr. Mary Lowe, recently concluded a three year national consultation on spiritual formation in online Christian education funded by a grant from the Wabash Center for Teaching and Learning in Theology and Religion. Dr. Lowe is involved in institutional assessment and accreditation activities with the Southern Association of Colleges and Schools and the Association of Theological Schools in the United States and Canada. During the last several years his institutional duties have increasingly taken on administrative responsibilities but he continues to teach online courses through the Erskine Virtual Campus. He has been teaching and administering in online education since 1995 and has served at Erskine Seminary for the last 15 years. Steve and Mary make their home in Due West, South Carolina.

Meri MacLeod, Ph.D. is a seasoned and sought after educator, both nationally and internationally. As a veteran leader she successfully created a distance program at a residence-only campus established for over a century. Established on the basis of quality standards her leadership guided the new distance program to national respect uncommon in graduate theological education. Meri introduced non-formal educational elements for community and interactive learning that fostered unprecedented retention rates for distance programs.

Starting from the ground up she coached faculty and students through their successful online transition and created new models of assessment. Her work included the development of effective support systems that reduced or eliminated common distance program costs while increasing student, staff, and faculty satisfaction. In 2007, Meri was one of eight theological educators chosen to participate in a three-year grant funded study on spiritual formation in distance learning. Her publications on online and distance learning appeared in the accrediting agency's professional publication, Theological Education and are available at www.digitalseminarian. com/resources.

Through Digital Seminarian, www.digitalseminarian.com, Dr. MacLeod brings her twenty years as an educator and academic administrator to her work of coaching, consulting, and training with specialties in faculty development, learning with technology, learning assessment and new program development. As dean of a 900-student program, she developed effective new administrative structures that reduced costs and increased enrollment. Her administrative experience is now applied to leading an international Christian school consortium that utilizes leading technology for 21st century learning while reducing the expected costs dramatically. The consortium is a growing community of practice for Christian educators working to integrate technology more effectively for learning. She can be reached at merim@digitalseminarian.com

C. Damon Osborne, Ph.D. serves as the Chair of the Graduate Education Department and the Assistant Vice President of Online Education at Mount Vernon Nazarene University. He has worked extensively in the field of professional development and teacher training, and has developed meaningful training opportunities in order to appropriately prepare prospective online instructors. Damon's research interests are focused primarily on the construction of community within the online learning environment.

Damon has written and presented on the topic of developing and fostering of a community of faith among online learners, relating both tools and techniques that allow online participants the ability to bridge the distance that can be found in the online learning environment.

David Morgan Phillips, D. Min. serves as the dean for the College of Lifelong Learning at Trevecca Nazarene University in Nashville, TN. He has assisted many colleges, universities, and seminaries as a consultant in online education, adult education, assessment, and accreditation. Phillips received his B.A. from Point Loma Nazarene University, M.A. and M.Div. from Azusa Pacific University, M.A.E.D. in adult education and distance learning from the University of Phoenix, M.S.E.D. in instructional design for online learners from Capella University, and D.Min. from Fuller Theological Seminary.

Prior to his current assignment, Phillips spent 25 years as a pastor and 13 years as the vice-president for online academic services at Nazarene Bible College in Colorado Springs, CO. He is married to Chris and has three children; Kim, Danny, and David Wesley.

Steven Lowell Yates, Ph.D. is Associate Dean for Biblical Enrichment and iLEAD Administration at Lancaster Bible College's iLEAD Center. Steve is excited about the opportunity to use alternative delivery systems to impact local churches and organizations around the World to fulfill the Great Commission. He completed his PhD at The Southern Baptist Theological Seminary studying leadership and Christian higher education. His research focus was faculty development for alternative delivery systems in Christian higher education.

Steve has served active duty on the seas and overseas in the United States Navy, worked for Prudential and IBM in corporate American as a database and systems designer, served as a Minister of Administration and Outreach for a local church, directed the purchasing and contracts as a director of procurement for Southern Seminary, and managed a LifeWay Christian Bookstore.

Steve lives in Lancaster, PA with his beautiful wife Lisa, and his amazing children James, Raymond, and Lauren. He enjoys running, reading, new technology, and playing with his chocolate lab Ruth.